SOMETIMES
YOU
HAVE
TO
SWITCH
OFF
THE
LIGHT

TO GET
YOUR
LIGHTBULB
MOMENT

YOU, ONLY BETTER

Nicholas Bate

Original illustrations by the author

CAPSTONE
A Wiley Brand

Registered office
John Wiley and Sons Ltd, The Atrium, Southern Gate, Chichester, West Sussex, PO19 8SQ, UK

For details of our global editorial offices, for customer services and for information about how to apply for permission to reuse the copyright material in this book please see our website at www.wiley.com.

Library of Congress Cataloging-in-Publication Data

Bate, Nicholas.
    You, only better / Nicholas Bate.
        pages cm
ISBN 978-0-85708-472-9 (pbk.)
1. Self-actualization (Psychology)   2. Self-realization.   I. Title.
BF637.S4B3844 2013
158.1–dc23

2013027654

A catalogue record for this book is available from the British Library.

ISBN 978-0-857-08472-9 (pbk) ISBN 978-0-857-08471-2 (ebk) ISBN 978-0-857-08469-9 (ebk)

Cover design by Mackerel ltd
Original illustrations by Nicholas Bate
Page design by Touchmedia (www.touchmedia.uk.net)
Set in ITC Officina and ITC Flood
Printed in Great Britain by TJ International Ltd, Padstow, Cornwall, UK

Contents

Introduction

You've noticed it and it's marvellous: that version of you which is you at your best: clear focus, bags of energy and a sense of humour. Creative, able to solve any challenge and brilliant at working with others. Confident but not arrogant, happy to say 'no' and go home on time and able to switch off easily at the weekend. Working on some exciting long-term plans, not worrying about money and yet keeping all the background stuff flowing well, too.

Yes, there is a version of you which is amazing. Unfortunately, for many of us, it is not only transient – appearing and disappearing apparently at whim – we have no idea how to access it.

There is a *You, Only Better*.
This book will show you how to find the best version of you and hang on to him or her. He/she is not as elusive as you think: a few simple shifts, perhaps a bit of additional knowledge and one or two fresh ways of thinking and you'll have that even better version of you.

Each chapter covers a major strand of the quest, e.g. being at your best. It'll give you easily implemented ideas, answer your toughest questions and share how someone else tackled the same problem. The book is eminently practical: we'll keep coming back to the challenges of being busy and of needing to squeeze change into an already busy lifestyle. There'll be nothing weird or that will require expenditure. *You, Only Better* is just a few simple ideas and shifts away.

Read on...

YOU, ONLY BETTER • *SECTION 1* $\longrightarrow$

DO WHAT YOU ARE BEST AT

How do you create the Perfect Life? In many ways of course: that's what this book is about. But at the *heart of it all* is to do what you are best at. And although on some days and in some moods it seems a no-brainer, it's worth just thinking about why...

1. Whatever you are best at tends – for you, not necessarily for everybody else – to be really enjoyable. And that reduces stress, makes it easier to leap out of bed in the morning and means you can maintain the highest standards of what you deliver.

2. If it's what you are best at, then you'll likely be better at it than most: you will be good at it and that means you can charge a sensible price for your skill.

3. When you are really good at something you tend only to get better. And that's good because you get more enjoyment out of it, you pull further ahead of the crowd and that protects your career.

4. If it's what you are best at, it will seem less like work and all those work/life balance issues which many people talk about will simply disappear for you.

But hang on a minute, you say. I'm best at five-a-side football, she's awesome at accounts and book-keeping and he just loves chatting to people and I think he could sell anything! So, what are we 'best at'? Football, accounts and selling respectively? I mean, maybe the latter two will work but I'm never going to get a job as a professional footballer. Never. And don't you dare give me any of that 'positive thinking' stuff. You see, I just don't get it. Not <u>everybody</u> can do what they are best at. There are already too many coffee shops and for that matter, too many management consultants. I could go on. So?

You make a good point and I'm glad you made it now because doing what you are 'best at' is not always obvious. No not at all. And I'm with you: it's certainly not as simplistic as 'positive thinking' yourself into a job as a TV chef simply because you make a mean lasagne. Surprisingly it's not necessarily as simple as doing what you are good at, doing what you can do easily, or even doing what people admire. So let's step back a bit and get some clarity.

What do we really, really mean by 'best at'?

'Best at' is a subtle mix of three things:

1. Firstly, you have a definite pull, a definite attraction to that skill, that activity and that way of spending your time: it's at the core of who you are. You feel you 'have' to do it. Football, solving problems, fiddling with technology, playing with ideas, knowing what's going on in the world of politics, drawing, inspiring people, writing … you name it, it's your thing. You feel very comfortable with it and curiously you are far less aware of time passing when you are 'doing that thing'.

2. Secondly, it is potentially marketable: it's a skill out of which <u>you</u> can make money. Note: maybe you couldn't at the moment, but there is the possibility. This might initially seem to put a damper on your love and timeless enjoyment of knitting and sewing. Not at all. The market for hand-produced unique garments is growing all the time, you simply need to multiply this love with a few easily learnt marketing and pricing skills to identify your target market.

3. And thirdly, *you* know this is your thing and not just because everybody else is doing it or because it's the latest fad. Nobody has told you: no parent, no careers adviser. This is *your* thing. Fancy a bit of jargon? You are *internally referenced* rather than *externally referenced*. This latter point is important because the only person who is going to make this plan come together is you. If it's simply what your mum wants, it'll fall down at some point. But if you are internally referenced, i.e. it is driven by you, it has a high likelihood of success. And this frustrates you because you *don't really know*. You know what you don't want to do. You are like most of us, then. But get on the path and you *will know*.

'Best at', therefore, is not always obvious at first glance. It is not always what you initially seem to be good at. It may surprisingly even be something you don't know that you are skilled at. Yet. It may have to evolve over time.

Doing what you are best at is just as much the path as the destination.

So – even though everybody rates Tim as one of the best five-a-siders on the planet, are you saying that may not be his thing? But surely Emille is OK; after all everybody needs book-keeping and accounts, don't they? And Firdou: well he could sell sand to the ... well, you know.

Yep, I am saying that. I'm saying that finding what you're best at and creating your own personal marketable skill is the win-ning strategy. But I am also saying it is not obvious and it is not easy. Absolutely possible and open to all of us. But it's not some quick-fix positive think strategy. Which is actually why most people don't really get to this stage. Not that they haven't got a personal best marketable skill, but they haven't given it the consideration that it justifies. After all: getting on a quest for doing what you are best at has got to be worth it!

How do I find out what that is for me?

BOUNCE

NOT JUST FOR BALLS

Alright then, I sort of get it. But how do I find out what my personal best marketable skill is if it's not as simple as 'what I enjoy' or 'what I am good at'? How does anyone?

It needs a bit of work and a bit of reflection and digging. Not much, but a little. And of course it is really worth it. There are three simple steps. Why don't we go through it generally and then explore your situation and that of Emille just as examples. Our three simple steps are (1) wake up, the one where we stop sleep-walking – hoping – and start to think about this important topic, (2) get real, where we apply some day-to-day and commercial common sense to what might be truly viable and (3) take action, the one where we stop talking and start doing.

Step 1: Wake Up to the Idea. Once you wake up to the idea that you do not have to do what you are currently doing, you do not have to do what causes you constant and consistent resentment, things begin to fall into place. You see before we have this 'ahhhaaa!' moment we tend to go along in a bit of a rut. Same old, same old and worst of all we stop thinking. We clutch at the straws of winning the lotto, 'one day' and the fantasy of doing 'our thing' such as – with all respect –'five-a-side'. Now you're awake you need to start observing. Get hold of an old-fashioned paper notebook and you need two running columns for the working day: what enlivens you, i.e. what you enjoy doing, what keeps you awake, makes you feel valuable, what almost, at times, you'd do even if you weren't being paid. And what is debilitating: what drains your energy, for which pay is a very important compensation. Keep this filled during the day. Here are some examples for Emille:

ENLIVENING	DEBILITATING
✓ WORKING WITH NUMBERS	✗ E-MAIL
✓ CREATING COMPLEX SOPHISTICATED SPREADSHEETS	✗ MEETINGS
✓ REPORTING TO THE SENIOR MANAGEMENT TEAM	✗ COMMUTING 2H EACH WAY
✓ & GETTING THEM TO UNDERSTAND A SUBTLE POINT	✗ OFFICE POLITICS

But, you say: it depends. Some meetings I enjoy, those with my team or which are well run for example. Fair point: we are assuming the debilitating effect is 'the event' rather than the fact that they are badly run. The latter can be fixed, the former needs to be attended to. And if it helps you can eventually prioritise the two columns.

Step 2: Get Real. Now take a long hard look at that enlivening column. Could you make a career out of them? Could you make a career out of them and drop some of the debilitating factors? The answer is probably for Emille a 'yes'. And that's the principle. But what will we do with Tim and his five-a-side which doesn't look too promising? Well, we can solve that too and we will soon. Now clearly there is a lot more we need to do, but that is the principle.

Step 3: Take Action. Stop talking about this and start doing some work. This might mean for Emille, going for a conversation about how to get promotion to allow her to focus more on what she enjoys and less on what she doesn't. It might mean having some challenging conversations with her boss in order to remove some of the 'debilitators'. It might even mean going out on her own and starting her own business. Let's return to Emille and Tim in more detail and understand how this discovery of what we are best at really works.

But First:

Isn't it simply a bit of luxurious thinking in a challenging world?

We live and work in challenging times. Isn't a bit luxurious to be thinking like this?

Perhaps, but how about if we realise it is actually the ONLY way to a sustainable career, the only way to keep our sanity. The only real way to build up our finances for later life? Things are not going to change. This is the new world of work: increasing austerity, global competitors and more automation and less need for people.

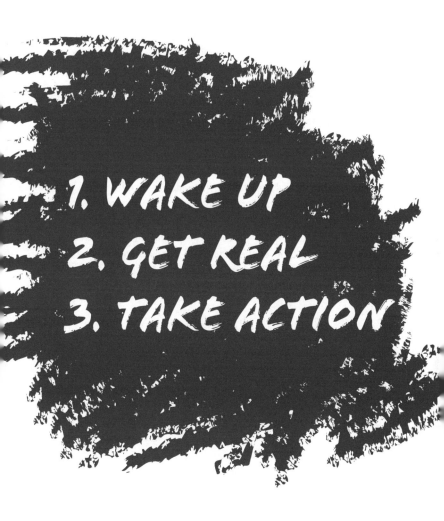

1. WAKE UP
2. GET REAL
3. TAKE ACTION

Tim

So, Tim. Tim currently works in IT. Has done since he left university. He's actually pretty good at it but hates the job. His real passion, as I think we have discovered, is five-a-side football. And playing that a couple of times a week plus the pub afterwards really gets him through the week. He knows he's unlikely to get promotion as he is always seen as a bit of a management challenge. To be honest he's pretty fed up and that is why he is constantly fantasising about creating a job out of his football.

The first thing for Tim on his quest to do what he loves, to do what he's best at, is to get the football stuff out of his head for a while. He's pretty well lived and breathed it since he was a child. It got him through school, got him through college and makes his working days palatable. He's also good. But would he really want to do it for the rest of his days? Not really. Nah, it was just that it was all he knew really. And being honest he'd never tried that hard at anything else. The lads liked a good footballer as did plenty of the girls. But maybe now at 27 he needed to start thinking a little differently. So:

Step 1: Wake Up. OK: his first big challenge: he's been sleep-walking through life a lot recently. Enough with the bullsh*t! Time to start taking this seriously. He borrowed a notebook from his girlfriend (he tended never to actually write anything down) and created the two columns. The first morning on the way to work he stopped in his favourite Starbucks, grabbed a drink and a table and attempted to complete the columns. He drew a blank. Maybe he didn't like anything? Maybe he was an absolute no hoper? Heck, this was depressing. But he sat there and eventually a surprising thought struck him: he actually did like solving IT problems. There it went!

ENLIVENING	DEBILITATING
✓ SOLVING (IT) PROBLEMS	-

And it was more than that, he liked being good at something and people needing his help and he liked helping them. Down it went:

ENLIVENING	DEBILITATING
✓ SOLVING (IT) PROBLEMS	-
✓ HELPING PEOPLE	-
✓ BEING RESPECTED	-

Funnily enough the debilitators were not flooding to mind as he might have thought they would have done; he was really enjoying this clarity. Anyway time to get to work.

For Tim, that became his morning ritual and by Friday he had this:

ENLIVENING	DEBILITATING
✓ SOLVING (IT) PROBLEMS	✗ NOT BEING APPRECIATED
✓ HELPING PEOPLE	-
✓ BEING RESPECTED	-
✓ BEING INCREDIBLY FAST TO RESPOND	-
✓ CREATING BREAKTHROUGH SYSTEMS WHICH SAVED TIME AND MONEY	-
✓ BEING AUTONOMOUS	-

This was good. This was going well. And the breakthrough had been on the debilitating side: not being appreciated.

Step 2: Get Real. Now could he make a career out of any of this? Well absolutely. There were now some threads to this thinking. One was to go freelance with his IT skills. A more radical one was to take his love of sport and problem solving and put them together and become some kind of fitness coach. An even more radical one was to develop a portfolio career where three days a week he did IT and two days fitness.

Step 3: Take Action. He was going to:
1. Work every morning on his plan.
2. Work even harder at work. That was good for work but also good for his skill set.
3. Stop fantasising about football as an escape but to think about it as a possible mini business.
4. Decide to launch his own thing in about 18 months.

EINSTEIN'S BLACKBOARD

$E = MC^2$

WHAT'S ON YOURS?

Emille

Emille is currently working in finance for a chain of cinemas in Paris. She too hates the job but loves numbers. A perfect spreadsheet is 'her thing'. She is brilliant at identifying the strategic and pertinent points from masses of data and tries to advise her management team appropriately. Unfortunately, they seem to be constantly making decisions by looking at apparently 'obvious' points such as high cost, but as Emille has tried to point out, these are just symptoms of a deeper problem ... Unfortunately she is aware that she is often ignored as 'just a girl from accounts' and what would she know about strategy?! She has thought about doing a 'distance-learning' MBA but they would not fund it and she also doesn't really need it: it would just look good on her CV.

Again, the first stage for Emille is to get all the old baggage and history out of her head. Sure she loves numbers and sure she finds a lot of the 'people stuff' a pain. But, on the other hand, she does enjoy convincing people of a strategic direction using the power of evidence. She also needs to let go of a lot of the 'everybody is against me' stuff. They're not: they simply haven't been sensitive to the fact that they have a real asset in their midst. Only Emille can change that.

Step 1: Wake Up. Analysis was her thing, so filling in a notebook was no problem at all. What was a problem for Emille was getting her to think differently with a fresh eye about what was really happening in her job.

ENLIVENING	DEBILITATING
✔ WORKING WITH NUMBERS	✘ E-MAIL
✔ CREATING COMPLEX SOPHISTICATED SPREADSHEETS	✘ MEETINGS
✔ REPORTING TO THE SENIOR MANAGEMENT TEAM	✘ COMMUTING 2H EACH WAY
✔ & GETTING THEM TO UNDERSTAND A SUBTLE POINT	✘ OFFICE POLITICS

Step 2: Get Real. It might initially be tempting to see a management consultant profile for Emille, but one of the things which is crucial for her is stability, and although going out on her own does not prohibit that at all, maybe it's not her first step. So, perhaps she needs to be re-engineering her role within the organisation?

Step 3: Take Action. Emille decided to:
1. Start keeping a portfolio of her successes.
2. Ask for a pitch to the management team to show how she might significantly increase her contribution.
3. Even if there is no salary increase for a while until she has proven her worth.
4. Her ultimate aim is a senior, strategic position with part-time help to cover some of her more administrative jobs.
5. She is excited about this.

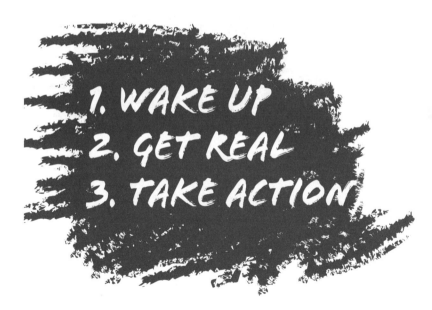

1. WAKE UP
2. GET REAL
3. TAKE ACTION

(IN CASE YOU MISSED IT BEFORE).

IT WAS DARK AND DEPRESSING IN HER CUBICLE

SO
SHE
GOT
UP.
STRETCHED.
AND
RE-STARTED
HER
LIFE.

YES, JUST LIKE THAT.

Top Tips

As you start to implement your **Wake Up; Get Real; Take Action** plan here are some straightforward tactics which will help you:

1. **Rock Star Good.** Decide to become Rock Star Good, i.e. really, really good at what you do, and aim to do this with as many aspects of your job as you can over time. E-mail is a pain if you don't have a system. If you dread the monthly presentation to the board it will cast a shadow over much of your job: decide to become really good at doing that presentation. Who knows where it might lead? We keep coming back to this point: don't be seduced by the obvious, the childhood dream, the hobby. Get good at what you do now and what you are best at **will** be revealed and you can begin to follow that path.

2. **There is a Threshold.** There is a point at which mastery can be gained in any task and with that mastery comes enjoyment. Thus simply work at becoming good at what you *have* to do as this may well reveal what you *want* to do. Notice how we have it the wrong way around so often, i.e. wanting to do something at which we have no prowess. There will be one or two who simply know in their deepest soul that they have to be a ballet star, but for most of us: get good, create mastery and enjoy doing what you are best at.

3. **Do It For You.** It's sometimes tempting to think: why bother? Organisations which don't appreciate you. Career paths which seem to have met a dead-end. Remember: do it for you. Doing what you are best at is not some 'end of the rainbow fantasy'. Do it really well, NOW. You will enjoy your day more. You will discover more about yourself. It will help your career. You will have more choices open to you.

4. **I vs. They.** One thing to get really good at it is taking ownership of your own destiny. Of not blaming others. Of not complaining about things which are out of your control. Life isn't always fair. And organisations are certainly not. You can get a discussion with your boss. You can save money for the course. You can watch less TV and read some books on the topic.

5. **You Will Change and Grow.** That's not a problem: it's what you want. The 'perfect life' sees you growing because that's what we are meant to do. Through growth we feel fulfilled. Do not be concerned that just when you get that strategic marketing position at your firm, you start becoming so good at it you feel like going out on your own. And then two years later you want to start talking about it and writing about it and want to get an academic position so you can do more research. That's brilliant. That's Life. That's doing what you are best at.

LOADS
MORE
HELP
IN THE FUTURE CHAPS.

A Few Questions If I May?

1. Somehow my case doesn't seem as 'simple' as the ones you have illustrated? I've tried the exercise but it hasn't really taken me very much further with my thinking.

Give it more time. Everybody gets there. Everybody else's case seems simpler. But do remember we may have been thinking in different ways for a decade or more. This exercise can take a bit of time to seep in. But it will eventually. And by all means continue reading this book, e.g. the chapters on creativity or making decisions which come later will undoubtedly 'spark' the breakthrough if it hasn't come already.

2. Nowhere here do you talk about the risks of chasing or following your dream. Some jobs may be dull but at least they pay the rent.

All jobs have risks, very few jobs are 100% secure any more. Your job, your career is increasingly what you make of it. And the best way to get 'security' is to do that about which you are passionate. No job is ever sustainable 'just because of the money'. So are you actually taking a risk by wishing to do what you are best at, or as you express it 'chasing your dream'? No, definitely not. There is much more risk in not finding that place in life.

3. Surely all jobs have their less attractive aspects. But that's life: we can't run away from everything we don't like.

There are a few things here. All jobs are riddled with the efforts of those who are less than professional, e.g. the manager who runs long, boring, unstructured meetings. Agreed – that's not something to run away from: that's something to address. But there are some people who just don't want to spend their days in meetings however brilliantly run they might be. That's what we're talking about here. And with effort and consideration they do have that choice. And with a 'Rock Star Good' mentality the few meetings they do need to run or attend can become tolerable, even enjoyable.

And Now Back to You

1. **This is important to you:** little can compare to the critical nature of getting on the right path for your career, so *slow down enough* that you can give it due consideration. Due attention. Due TLC.

2. **Keep a notebook** – *for weeks if necessary* – of 'enliveners', those activities, tasks and ways of spending time which make you feel good, are often timeless and (*secretly of course*) you might even do for free. And also of the 'debilitators', those things which make you lose energy, which you hate and almost no amount of money can really get you to enjoy.

3. **Be honest about what you want to do.** Many people will have advice on what you *should do* to be happy, wealthy etc. Listen to their advice of course, but ultimately the decision must be driven by you. 'Shoulds' are rarely sustainable.

4. **Remember,** the path to success is a combination of an enlivener and something which is commercially viable and comes from you. There will be a successful combination there.

5. **The core strategy** is wake up/get real/take action.

6. **Explore,** and in the quest for something which is commercially viable, play with multipliers, i.e. it is not one thing (loving technology) but the fact that you love technology and you love precision drawing which might lead you into graphic design.

7. **Now create a plan to make this happen.** If you are worried about having the energy to make this happen or where to find the time or how to get some creative thoughts and which choices to make … that's all coming up in future chapters. And a lot more.

8. Remember the key tips to use on the path:

   (a) **Rock Star Good.** Decide to become Rock Star Good, i.e. really, really good at what you do and aim to do this with as many aspects of your job as you can over time.

   (b) **There is a Threshold.** There is a point at which mastery can be gained in any task and with that mastery comes enjoyment.

   (c) **Do It For You.**

   (d) **I vs. They.** One thing to get really good at is taking ownership of your own destiny.

   (e) **You Will Change and Grow.** That's not a problem: it's what you want.

9. So: start the process of getting on the quest to be the best version of you.

10. Read on!

THAT BUSINESS COLOUR CHART IN FULL

 HIGHLIGHTER YELLOW

 PPT INCOMPREHENSION BLACK

 POOR QUARTER RESULTS TEARS BLUE

 NEW LOGO RED

 COFFEE BRAND GREEN

 FEEL-THE-QUALITY BUS. CARD OFF WHITE

 MONDAY MORNING MEETING GREY

 CEO PERSONAL PARKING SPACE REGAL BLUE

YOU, ONLY BETTER • **SECTION 2** $\longrightarrow$

BEING AT YOUR BEST

If you are reading this book in chapter order then you will notice that there is a logical sequence to creating a whole new better you: clearly, what you are doing – *your job, vocation, career* – is an excellent starting place. But it does raise one issue: energy.

(Of course if you have just dived into this chapter thinking it's the one you need most, that's fine. It works perfectly well stand-alone.)

You see it's obvious from the last chapter that although none of it is that complicated, it does require a bit of 'oommph': putting aside a bit of reflection time, maybe doing some internet research and perhaps having some tricky conversations with a boss. **It requires energy**. But for so many people there is no spare energy: from the time the alarm goes off until they collapse into bed at night it's a sequence of things which 'need to be done', from answering e-mails to picking up the kids from school to hoping for some TV time and perhaps a glass of wine, but no real time to do anything different. Anything new. Or to be truthful, no real energy to make any changes. We *will* touch on time management later, but it really starts with *energy* management.

ENERGY

CREATIVITY

PASSION

FOCUS

LOVE OF
LIFE

GETTING
STUFF DONE

ALL INDICATORS WERE
DANGEROUSLY LOW.

SHE NEEDED A DEEP REST.
AND SOON

And to get that energy, we sort of know what to do: we *should* probably take more exercise, we *should* probably eat better and we *should* probably not get so stressed. But it's easier said than done ... and all those 'shoulds' are such a pain ... All right: let's first look at what would be useful to have more energy for and then perhaps *even* more usefully see how we can make it happen, EASILY!

Strategies for Being at Our Best

Understand that there are **two kinds of personal energy**: there is the *physical* kind, we literally feel strong and could stride out across Paris, even though the metro is down, to get to the exhibition we would like to see. And then there is *mental* energy, having the ability to push back on the bullying client. The two are clearly inter-linked. If you are feeling physically strong it tends to give you mental 'stamina'. And if you have clarity and strength of thought you tend you feel physically better. But from the point of view of improving them, it's good to look at them separately and then it's easier to make adjustments. Let's start with physical and move on to mental.

Getting back your physical energy

Physical Tip 1: Get physically fit. You would have guessed this one wouldn't you? Clearly exercise creates a strong body. The investment you make pays back many times over. But reaching that initial threshold, where we feel that the return on the investment has been a good one, is for many of us a tough step. Yes it is a good idea to go the gym, to swim, to play tennis. But: where do we get the time? And how do we stop those first sessions being so painful? What do we need to actually do? And then, once we get going, how do we stop the boredom?

ALTHOUGH
THE
BOXING
BAG
HAD
A
SWAGGER,
HE
KNEW
WHO
WOULD
WALK
AWAY
THAT
FINE SUNDAY MORNING

1. *Getting the time*: initially try not to look for big chunks of additional time, simply build it into your day with two very easy ways to accumulate additional cardiovascular energy: walk and take the stairs. Most people come across plenty of sets of stairs in their day-to-day work. But increasingly they avoid these by using the escalator or the lift. Don't: use the stairs. You are on floor 17? Alright: take the lift up, but walk down at lunch-time. The car has now become the default mode of transport where once it was walking. Start walking. Neither process will take more time. Walking in particular allows time for reflection, means you don't have to find anywhere to park and is sometimes much more flexible for short, multi-stop journeys. Once you have walking and 'the stairs' built into your way of being your body will want to do more. At which point you will be perfectly happy to start swimming or tennis or gym circuits.

2. *Stopping the pain*: pain is simply bad practice. It's doing too much too soon, which is why walking and stairs are a brilliant way in. Once that is easy and not causing breathlessness, look to stretch your capacity. Raise your heart rate and/or lift additional weights. But there is no need for pain: start small, start slowly. But start.

3. *What do I actually need to do*: for physical fitness? There are three considerations. There is CV or cardiovascular. That's your breathing and your heart of course. The goal for most of us is to strengthen and protect our heart and improve our breathing and thus our lung capacity. Your local council gym or your doctor will be able to do an initial assessment which you can then aim to improve on. Then there is work to improve muscle strength. You could assess this yourself by a simple test, such as the number of press-ups or steps you can do in a certain period of time, but a gym assessment will be a bit more scientific. And then – often forgotten – there is posture, core strength and keeping the body integrated. Your local gym may do Pilates classes which will teach you how to keep your body connected. If that seems a bit of a daft concept, notice how many people at the gym will, say, just work on arm muscles, but eventually become unbalanced and are leaning forward all the time. If you easily and consistently work on all three they will reinforce each other; thus if posture is

good then muscles will have more effect; if lung capacity is excellent then muscles can build more rapidly. And the more subtle effect is of course the connection with mental energy: imagine how much 'better' you feel if your posture is excellent.

4. *Eliminating boredom*: seek variety. If you are basically happy with the gym approach, keep varying your routine. Ask for advice. If you go swimming, try adding some cycling. If you are tennis player, what about some squash? Variety is not just good for us in maintaining motivation, it is good for the body in ensuring no muscles get ignored and all muscles are constantly stretched to a higher performance.

Physical Tip 2: Eat better. For most of us reading this, food is now so plentiful that we have begun to get confused between food for fuel and food for nutrition. Driving along the motorway snacking on crisps and a can of soda balanced on the passenger seat might stop us collapsing but will not necessarily do anything for our long-term well-being and energy. Because such foods are mostly empty calories: they lack much nutrition. And because they are only satisfying in an addictive kind of way (the way when you have had a few crisps you must have more) it's so very easy to overeat. But the messages are so conflicting and there are so many weird diets, what do I need to eat? And how come so much junk food tastes so great? And how do I stop myself eating too much?

But what's 'good'? After all there are so many conflicting messages out there? There are indeed. Everybody has 'their thing' and at any particular time there is usually a diet which everybody swears by. But talk to your doctor, do your own research, look for the commonality across healthy diets all over the world and you will find agreement that the body needs:

1. *Oxygen*. Yes, perhaps a bit surprising to express it in those terms, but it is our primary fuel. Get up and move around as often as you can. Sitting poorly in a chair staring at a screen for hours on end is not that conducive to feeling fantastic.

2. *Water*. Around 2 litres a day. Simply alternate it with your other drinks of choice. That will ensure less sugar and caffeine and more simple water and better hydration.

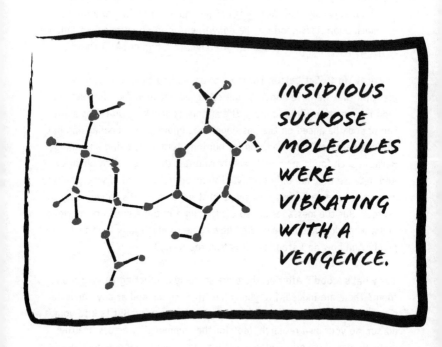

INSIDIOUS SUCROSE MOLECULES WERE VIBRATING WITH A VENGENCE.

3. *Complex carbohydrates rather than simple sugars*. Pastas and potatoes and good quality breads provide a steady, more satisfying flow of energy than the quick fix of two teaspoons of sugar thrown into a mug of coffee.

4. *Protein*. Wherever you are on the eating scale (omnivore ... vegan) you will be getting enough protein.

5. *Fruit and vegetables*. But it is highly likely that you are not getting enough fruit and vegetables. Choose and eat more.

And how come so much junk food tastes so good? It's one of those features from early in our evolution. Remember that the body has plenty of mechanisms to encourage us to think short-term and focus on our immediate survival. We taste something sweet: our brain suggests *'lets eat lots of that as we never know when we might get some more'*. Of course early in our history when we might not have come across more food for a while it was a great strategy. Fortunately most of us know exactly when we can get some more – just by opening the fridge – and it need not be now. As you switch to healthier foods they will taste good and highly processed foods will taste ... well ... processed. Just give it time.

And how do I stop myself eating too much? If this is a challenge for you then you will no doubt have had many strategies suggested to you, from using smaller plates to never eating alone to ... And these are all well and good. But perhaps one which you haven't really utilised before is an integrated approach: in other words, don't necessarily focus on eating less, but do focus on getting better sleep, taking some exercise, reducing anxiety etc. Because eating too much is often to compensate for missing areas in our life: not feeling grounded, not feeling well. Complete those areas and the desire to eat beyond what we really need falls away.

Physical Tip 3: Get enough sleep. And ensure it is quality sleep. Sleep is clearly the definitive physical booster, the definitive provider of energy: we all know that when we are well rested and have slept well we are invincible, but equally after just a few broken nights the coffee has to start flowing and we become less and less effective. But what is enough sleep? And how do we stop ourselves not being able to fall asleep or waking up too early worrying about things?

What is enough sleep? When you wake naturally. Start exploring the possibilities of waking naturally, i.e. without an alarm clock. Always set your alarm as a back-up, but aim to get enough sleep that you wake without needing it. It might take you a week or two of experimentation, of going to bed 15 minutes earlier (and the next night another 15 minutes earlier) until you find your nightly need, but it's well worth it.

How do I achieve good quality sleep? This is for you if you are not sleeping well:

1. Return the bedroom to a sanctuary: get rid of junk and do not allow it to double as a home office. Make it a calm and pleasant place to sleep deeply and peacefully.

2. Banish screens (TV, computers, phones) and stimulus (caffeine, alcohol) in the last few hours before bed.

3. Read a novel to get you drowsy.

4. If you wake in the night, sit up in bed, close your eyes and focus on your breathing and you will fall asleep.

Building up your mental energy

Mental Tip 1: Take time out. We live now in a very busy world. Most of us do more, travel more and work more than we did even a few years ago and we can expect that trend to continue. It's partly what our jobs require and partly what we aspire to. In addition we are 'on' much more of the time. We are checking mail, watching TV, updating Facebook, texting across the world. And it's all wonderful. But it does take its toll: we do not, after all, possess the 24/7 capabilities of the machines we use. You will have more physical energy if you take some time out and remove as

HER POWER RESOLUTION

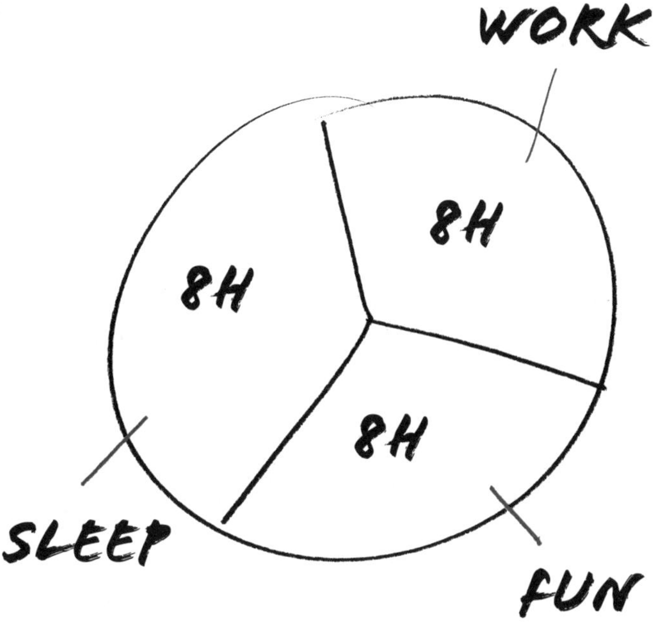

many distractions as you can. Take a walk and do nothing; don't check your phone, don't try and solve a problem, just be. Notice how 'enlivening' it is. Do more of that. Note that watching TV is not time out: it may be relaxing but there is still a large amount of data input. It's the latter you are looking to reduce.

Mental Tip 2: Spin it. Stuff happens, it really does. Some of it is in our control and we can learn from the result. Some of it is not in our control so we simply have to accept it. But the main thing is, little in our life is absolute, or putting it another way, we can 'spin' the way we look at something. Our not getting the job is not the end of the world. But it could be our learning to do more preparation next time. Or even that it wasn't a suitable job for us in the first place. Stuff happens and we can choose how we look at it, that is 'spin it'.

Mental Tip 3: De-clutter. There are many things which mentally energise us. Fresh stimulation of course; and for most people clarity. Especially gaining clarity. We tend to live a life where more gets added and little is taken away. At the start of our lives good parents hide some of the toys each play session, but as our lives progress we need to do that ourselves.

Mental Tip 4: Get out of your head. We noted earlier that mental and physical energies are strongly interconnected. Nowhere is this more true than with hand and head: we now tend to spend more and more of our time in our head. And to sometimes escape from it we get out of our head in inappropriate ways such as alcohol overload; a healthier route is to use our hands by making bread or learning to paint or doing more gardening. It can seem odd initially; you might not have dabbled with 'art' or clay or gardening or real cooking or knitting since you were a child; but persevere. Notice how therapeutic it can be. Keep it as simple as possible initially, e.g. with bread making avoid the bread-making machine: do it all by hand. Get out of your head.

Mental Tip 5: Real friends, real places, real time. A great friend in a real place. A great conversation. What could be more healing? More helpful? Virtual networking and friendship capabilities are marvellous. But nowhere near as good as the real thing: the deeper conversation rather than the sound bites of the blackboard. The physical presence rather than the irritations of Skype.

Mental Tip 6: What's the point? Get up. Go to work. Meet a friend. See a movie. Have a drink. Wake up. Go to work. Put lasagne in microwave. Write e-mail to tax people. Wake up. Go to work. What's the point? Sometimes we need a bigger perspective. Take a blank sheet of paper, turn it landscape, put today's date and add three years. Now draw how you want things to be. Notice the word is want. And yes: draw. Drawing avoids us falling into the clichés of words which we have used so many times, such as 'money', 'success', 'travel'. Now sleep on it for 48 hours before coming back and deciding on some action to get you close to this vision. To help us fight the daily battles in the swamp, we all need to spend some time on the mountain top.

Top Tips for Making it Happen

1. **Start small.** Everybody wants to get fit quickly, but doing too much too soon is likely to cause the pain which will just deter us from doing it regularly. Start small. Yes the body needs to be stretched but only within reason. If you are at the gym and notice others are working with heavier weights, or at greater inclines on the running machine, do not be tempted to copy: they worked up to it and so can you.

2. **Start slowly.** As point 1. Make your programme regular and frequent. If the exercise is manageable you will be tempted to return: create a timetable.

3. **Look for the snowball effect.** As you build frequency and momentum you will see cumulative effects. Your walking will improve your taking of the stairs which will improve your swimming which will improve your limb strength.

4. **Work at all aspects: they will reinforce each other.** Sleeping well will mean you need fewer 'snacks' to motivate you. Exercising will cause you to crave decent food. Taking time out will reduce the stress which causes addictive behaviours.

5. **There are no set-backs: just adjustments.** Having great energy is simply a journey. You will have set-backs, the most obvious one being that we occasionally fall unwell. Simply rest and recuperate and then get back on the path.

Katie and Ben

They don't know each other, although they live oddly parallel lives: Ben in London, UK. Katie in Sydney, Australia. Both are 27, both are high performers and both are single and not ready to settle down: career is all.

For Katie, her body is her temple. She's never not been fit. She loves fruit and vegetables and the Sydney lifestyle allows her to be incredibly active. Most mornings she runs from home to work via the harbour, a glorious and inspiring run. Several mornings a week it's Pilates class first thing at 7am and alternate lunch times it's yoga or kick boxing. The evenings are her free time with her friends when they usually end up in a bar. Until a year ago she always felt great. But over the last ten months it has been more and more of a struggle to get up and out for the morning run and she's frustrated that her sleep is not so good and that she just worries. She's a planner and if anything doesn't go to plan it stresses her so much.

It was a friend's comment that hit her hard: 'Katie: maybe you just need a bit more balance: not everything is a plan, you know'. This shocked her – after all she felt she was addressing that aspect of her life through her yoga. Of course it was true that she hated it when the teacher started late. She decided to cancel all her lunchtime classes and just enjoy her break and lunch and stop 'micro-scheduling' everything: she walked across the road to the park near the museum and ate her salad there. She also joined an evening pottery class. A couple of months later, Katie felt better than ever.

SOMETIMES
YOU
NEED
SPACE

AWAY
FROM
THE
MADDING
CROWD

For Ben the problem was more fundamental. He had simply stopped doing anything apart from work. Financial services was a tough sector and he was doing well in the sense that he was making great money and moving up the ladder rapidly. But he did spend a huge amount of his time sitting staring at a screen and tapping at a keyboard, and if he wasn't there he was sitting in a bar with a beer in one hand and his BlackBerry in the other. He felt pretty stressed most of the time, he ate fast/quick food at all meals and was only 'happy' when drinking. He had a wake-up call when a promotion necessitated a medical. The doctor was not impressed: every indicator, every simple measure was that of somebody thirty years older! He needed to change. But he had no time so he made three deals with himself: (1) walk the escalator on the London underground: he took them anyway so instead of just standing there he would walk them (2) stop taking cabs for tiny rides: just walk (3) and no alcohol Monday, Tuesday, Wednesday. He did that for one month and then joined a badminton class. OK: it was going to be a long and maybe slow recovery but not only was his breathing and energy so much better, he was once again feeling normal rather than wretched and just craving his next coffee or beer.

WITH

EXERCISE

IT

WOULD

GROW

A Few Questions If I May?

1. *I'm not sure you have really addressed the fact that some people such as me hate exercise. Always have, did so at school. Every so often I try a new thing: spinning class or even a personal trainer. Never works.*

Perhaps the biggest current barrier to you becoming fit again is the phrase 'I hate exercise' as if it is a given and that is the end of it. People change and you can change. You may well have got off to a bad start at school. Perhaps your spinning class and/or personal trainer were trying to get you to move too quickly. Humans are meant to be fit and feel good when they are fit. Of course, if we are out of practice it can take time. But start. The stairs and walking. You will be able to get fit.

2. *Decent food takes time to prepare: I don't have time. And I'm not sure instant meals are so bad for you.*

Many instant meals have a very simple and unadulterated list of ingredients: it would be inappropriate to say they are 'bad' for you. However they cannot be as good as grilling your own fish, boiling some new potatoes and steaming some green vegetables. The instant meal will not cover all the different food requirements you have, and if we just invest a little in the right utensils and a slight change to our evening routine it is much more satisfying to cook and eat one's own meal rather than tear open a packet.

3. *I just don't see how I am going to get any serious e-mail free time to 'chill': my job requires me to liaise with the USA. They know I am still awake at 9pm UK time: they want a response.*

OK: bear with me and let's discuss this more in Chapter 4 where we will look at good productivity practices.

And Now Back To You

1. **Energy management: that's what it's really about.**
   There is so much talk about 'I need to be better at time management in order get done what I want to achieve'. NO! Energy management first, then time management will fall into place.

2. **Energy comes from physical well-being AND mental well-being.** They support each other: work on both, little and often.

3. **Little and often is an easy strategy:** it overcomes time challenges. It avoids pain.

4. **For physical energy think about:** exercise, diet and sleep.

5. **For exercise:** walk and take the stairs. Once those are easy find a variety of exercises you enjoy.

6. **For diet:** think nutrition not (just) fuel.

7. **For sleep:** think back to basics: no screens, no caffeine, no work for the last few hours before bed ...

8. **For mental energy think about:** time out, bigger picture, spin it, de-clutter, get out of your head, real friends.

9. **For time out:** practise doing nothing and switching off.

10. **For bigger picture:** draw your vision and act upon it.

11. **For spin it:** look at 'the problem' in a healthier way, a more resourceful way.

12. **For de-clutter:** simplify your life. De-clutter physically and mentally.

13. **For get out of your head:** use your hands, e.g. make bread.

14. **For real friends:** spend real time in real places with real people.

YOU, ONLY BETTER • SECTION 3 ⟶

SET YOUR PERSONAL COMPASS

In the last chapter, how did you get on with the *'What's the point?'* exercise, the one with the piece of paper, drawing and three years from now? Hopefully it got you thinking, stretching your imagination and revealing some important actions for you to take for the longer term. We're going to take that exercise further and deeper in this chapter, so if you had any difficulties with it then this chapter should resolve them.

We live in a **clock** world: the focus is on time and date. And as we all get busier we make more and more reference to time and date, indeed we become slowly but surely sucked into a world of managing our time. We have already suggested that life is not really about time management, it's more about energy management. Here's a second suggestion: that once you have your energy boosted then you can sort out where you are headed; you can sort out your direction: or you can start setting your compass. Your **Personal Compass**.

- You may have optimised your day (time management) but what's the point if you never get any decent time with your family (direction management)?

- You may hit all your delivery targets (time management) but what's the point if you lose your health (direction management)?

Time management is often about getting stuff done. Direction management is about getting the right stuff done. Time management is about clock time, direction management is about compass time.

Clock time is critical. Catching our flight. Getting our dissertation in on time. Being at the nursery to pick up our son. Starting the board meeting punctually. But direction is critical too: where are we taking our business? What is the best schooling for our son? Compass time often gets lost in the addictiveness of clock time.

THE
LOCH NESS MONSTER
DIDN'T
ACTUALLY
NEED

EVERYBODY TO BELIEVE IN HIM

HE
BELIEVED
IN
HIMSELF

Personal Compass

Personal Compass is an idea I have used and evolved over many years of teaching. The analogy holds well: on a geographic compass, which used to be favoured by boy scouts and girl guides until GPS devices became the norm, there are of course four main directions: North, South, East and West. Clearly it doesn't matter how fast we travel East, if we are trying to get South – it isn't going to work. Direction needs to be set, maintained and regularly reviewed. We are now often so busy we just hope that the sheer speed of covering the terrain will get us to where we want to be. Sadly no: we need to be on the right road.

On our Personal Compass there are six main directions, two of which – Compass Points 1 (career) and 2 (wellness) – we have made some very good progress on already, so we can cover those briefly and then complete our compass with the other four. Very few people get around to setting their Personal Compass: you will. It'll give you focus, clarity and, obviously, direction.

Personal Compass Point 1: Career

Most people would say they want to be happy, of course. But what makes us happy? Money? A great holiday? Superb Belgian chocolate? A great movie? Having a free day? Time with the children? Time without the children?! All of these things of course. However, interestingly many of these are what we might call *blips* of happiness, i.e. they do cause us to feel happier, but not for long. Thus, if suddenly your organisation announced it had surprisingly closed an amazingly profitable business deal and everybody in the organisation was going to get an immediate bonus, and to make it more fun it would be given to you in cash and at the end of the day and you were given a discreet brown envelope full of £500 of cash, you'd be happier wouldn't you? Of course. But, longer term, that happiness would evaporate. After all, when you have a spare moment calculate the amount of money you have had in your working life to date: all of us should be ecstatic. What about a holiday? Same challenge. Fantastic to look forward to, fantastic to enjoy. And hopefully happy memories. But much of its 'happiness' effects are soon forgotten on a day-to-day basis.

Is there anything which does seem to cause long-term *accumulated* happiness: pure contentment if you like? Yes: our career and our relationships. With both of these, things can just keep getting better. So back to career.

That's what Chapter 1 was about of course; doing what you are best at, as it is the only sustainable strategy. It's not easy. It can take a long time to find what you are best at: it's not always at all obvious. But it is your first compass point.

Work/life balance

We'll not make a big fuss about it in this book, but one challenge some people talk about is their lack of 'work/life balance'. Typically they mean of course, too much work and not enough play. Setting your six compass points is a brilliant way of ensuring work/life balance: before you take the wonderful job in Inverness with its associated huge salary increase, what will be the implications for your family time? Setting the compass insists on answers to these important questions. As you work through the six compass points you'll be asked challenging questions of each, but not only that; you'll learn to bear in mind the implications for the other five and thus balance – although certainly never easy – can be maintained.

Time to look at the next compass point.

WHEN
INTERNATIONAL NEWS WAS GRIM,
SHE HAD ONE OR TWO PROBLEMS
OF HER OWN TOO
AND BUSINESS COULD BE BETTER

SHE WALKED,
BECOMING GROUNDED
ALWAYS HELPED

ONE DAY, ONE STEP AT A TIME
SHE HAD LEARNT

Personal Compass Point 2: Wellness

When we are well we feel balanced, grounded and we have clear focus. We can let the small stuff go. And of course we have energy, the topic of the last chapter. Just to reiterate, it is acquired through addressing both the physical body and the mental body. It can take time to rebuild both to the levels we would like and that means a small-step but steady approach.

There is no priority order to the Personal Compass points. We are certainly not saying career is more important that wellness, nor that those two are more important than the four we will be discussing in a moment. However, they are natural bedrocks for the other compass points.

Having reviewed the first two compass points, let's now take a look at the remaining four which we have not addressed at all, yet.

Personal Compass Point 3: Personal Finance

Ahh, personal finance. Mention this compass point to many and there is a sigh. And generally a sigh of slight despair. They know their finances are a mess. They are not quite sure how big a mess. They know they are not in control and that debt is costing them money; there is an anxiety about the long-term future. But they have no idea how to get out of the loop. Here's some help:

1. **Money never creates happiness.** The lack of money causes unhappiness. Ask any lotto winner: the money is fantastic to pay off debts and go on a holiday after five years of no holiday. But then? Most – *in order to stay sane* – go back to work. As we said earlier when discussing Personal Compass Point 1, a true source of happiness is what we do on a day-to-day basis: our career, our job, our vocation. Doing what we are best at, what we love: that's what gets us out of bed in the morning. Money is not a motivator, it is simply something which we need to ensure is not a blocker to what we really want to do. And although some people do set out to make loads of money and do succeed, the more common model is a non-financial drive; the drive to express themselves. To invent or run a better coffee shop or be a better designer of wedding dresses or ... And if it is their true passion, they will get good at it, and if they get good at it they can charge a sensible rate, and – you've guessed it – they will make money.

FROM ZERO TO HERO

2. All well and good, **but what if lack of money is causing us unhappiness?** Read on:

3. Back to Chapter 1: **get 'Rock Star Good' at what you do.** Whether you are a receptionist or a short-order chef or a public speaker, do it better. Do it to the best of your ability. There is always a demand for excellence and then you will have a secure career, be able to earn a good wage and your money problems will become manageable. It's true that not everybody will appreciate your hard work, not everybody will notice how good you are, that some people will abuse and take advantage of your efforts, that it will take longer to 'break through' than you would like, that at times it will seem that you will never get to a position where your value is being appreciated. But you will.

4. **Act as you wish to be perceived.** Act like a leader even though you do not yet have manager in your job title, act as if this were your coffee shop in the way you treat the customers even though you just clear tables and are on the minimum wage. Pay for some of your own training courses because the company you currently work for is too mean to invest in you. Believe in yourself, and here's the key: aim that people stop measuring you in terms of the time you are around, but the value you offer. If they just see you as so brilliant and useful to have around the coffee shop that when it is your day off it is close to a disaster. That yes, there are other team leads on the night shift but wow, only you can get 125% out of everybody. That's everybody, even the cynics. And once people see you in terms of value not time, you can start to be paid in terms of value not time.

5. And that is very exciting as if you are paid in terms of time, there is naturally a limit to how much you can earn. **But if you are paid in terms of value, there is no limit at all.**

6. **Understand wealth.** There are two kinds of wealth. There is soft wealth. That's a great job, great health. Brilliant friends. Unfortunately, they are often only valued when it is too late. Decide now to slow down, be in the moment more often and appreciate what you have, especially if it is 'free'. Too often when we are at work we are thinking about home. And when we are at home, we are worrying about work.

7. Then there is hard wealth. That is not your salary. Anybody can earn a high salary. The real question is: **what is your cost base?** Because if you are spending more than you are earning then you still have difficulties ahead. The true way to discover your worth, your wealth, is to evaluate your personal balance sheet, i.e. add up your assets and take away your liabilities. Ideally you would like that figure to be positive: of course it may be a well-managed negative for a while, perhaps because of a mortgage, but ultimately there comes a time when you would like to reach financial independence so that you do not need to work.

8. **Start counting again:** use cash whenever you can. Cash allows you to appreciate the value of things. The credit card and the swipe devices can very easily remove any kind of value consciousness and thus it is very easy to spend too much too often. That shirt, that bag of groceries, those premium seats at the cinema: all easily swiped, easily purchased by credit card. But with cash; do I really need that shirt? What can we leave out of our grocery shop this week? Heck, we don't need premium seats for goodness sake!

9. **Get a handle on the number,** i.e. the amount of money you need to reach financial independence. Nobody wants to discuss it with you: not your pension company, not your employer, not the government. Nobody knows the answer to the dilemma that everybody wants to work less, everybody wants a great standard of living, few really want to get their finances resolved and longevity is rapidly increasing. The sooner you work yours out, the sooner you can make sure you can achieve it.

10. And if much of the above makes you feel low, then **don't panic.** Here's the definitive tip.

11. **Chase quality of life rather than standard of living**. Standard of living is stuff: carpets, sofas, music systems. All fun, all good and all what many of us desire of course. But take care: if we become wedded to the god of 'stuff' we may find we simply need to work harder and harder and ironically the quality of our life goes down: so chase quality of life rather than standard of living.

Personal Compass Point 4: Relationships

Many things give us blips of happiness: money, a holiday, a great movie, a trip to the zoo, closing the deal. But only a few things give us long-term accumulative happiness. One is our career, being the best version of ourselves; doing what we love. And another is our relationships. Let's study the five 'A's of great relationships:

Attention: all relationships need attention if they are to thrive. Your client, your four-year-old daughter, your friend. Without attention your client will go elsewhere, your daughter may well withdraw and your friend will not be available when you need him/her. But the challenge is that attention differs from person to person. Your client doesn't want too much but would like to be involved in the strategy updates. Your daughter wants some silly time with dolls and duplo and doesn't want to be micro-scheduled between e-mail and supper time. Your friend wants texts replied to reasonably promptly. Attention is different for everybody ...

Awareness of difference: part of giving attention is meeting the different needs of another person. Your girlfriend wants peace and quiet for at least an hour when she gets home from work. She appreciates that you give her that time before expecting conversation. Some of your team are chatty contributors in the team meeting; some are quiet and reserved, but all have great ideas, it's just finding the best ways to get those ideas into the conversations. Diversity brings fun, fresh thinking and stronger teams. But it can also bring resentment, irritation, frustration and anger. Unless ...

Appreciation of difference: the quiet one says very little in the team meeting: we would like them to SAY something. But we might appreciate their deeper thinking and eventual powerful contributions. Why do we always end up tidying the kitchen first? But maybe our boyfriend is brilliant at doing the finances and keeping our debt down. Why can't your assistant simply be friendlier on the phone to clients? Although maybe he is really good at his reporting and hitting targets. Appreciate difference: it'll create a great team and it'll improve our personal relationships. This does not mean we have to excuse anybody's poor behaviour. Lateness is not about difference: it is simple rudeness.

HER LOCAL BARISTA WAS CUTE

HER DAILY FIX HAD SHIFTED
FROM CAFFEINE TO LOVE

Affection: and for our personal lives, always having time for those who are most important. Affection is being there and coping with the quirkiness of the person you fell in love with.

Act first: when a relationship isn't working, be the first to suggest we start talking again. It's not a sign of weakness, it's a sign of incredible strength.

Personal Compass Point 5: Fun

What's the point if you're not having fun? And here's where you'll begin to see the power of the Personal Compass. If you are doing what you are best at, what you are passionate about, then fun is more part of your everyday life and not something which requires money or alcohol. Fun is not something to put off to 'one day'. Fun is who we are as human beings. If you look after your wellness, you will naturally feel you are having fun just on a day-to-day basis. If you maintain your relationships then fun will be a lot easier.

Personal Compass Point 6: Contribution

Contribution or giving back. Yes we know we 'ought' to. But is that all this is about? An 'ought', something to feel guilty about? No, not at all. It's a perfect win–win, it's an important part of our compass. When we give back, we not only help our cause, be it the homeless, or overgrown canals or disadvantaged third-world children, we ourselves grow hugely. We discover who we really are. And that of course supports the other aspects of our compass.

Top Tips for Making it Happen

1. **Review it monthly.** Pick a key date in the month – pay day is an obvious one – and on that day review the compass. Review means check how each compass point is doing in isolation and how it is doing in connection to the other five points.

2. **Share it with those who are important.** Your partner in life, your children. Every person has their own compass. If you are sharing your life with someone, it is appropriate that your and their compass overlap each other. The compass is a brilliant way to articulate your hopes and your wishes. It is a brilliant way to support each other. It is a brilliant way to avoid surprises by highlighting changes in your thinking early on.

3. **Keep it integrated.** Always discuss all six compass points together. That will keep you grounded and in balance.

4. **Make it happen.** Identify the actions you need to take and note these on what we will call a Master List (ML). The next chapter will reveal more on this important point!

Hoshimi

Hoshimi had known for about 18 months that her life was increasingly chaotic. On her 30th birthday she had ended up miserably ill after a wild night out in her beloved home of Tokyo. But nursing her head on a quiet Sunday with a plate of KFC she knew things had to change. Her friend Sahiye said she would just need a long weekend away doing some shopping, but Hoshimi knew it was more fundamental than that. Her body couldn't take it any longer. And to be honest the thought of 48 hours' back-to-back shopping simply didn't appeal any more. Rather like the quick fix of the Kentucky Fried – their normal solution to alcohol abuse – it simply didn't appeal. She needed to get sorted and she dug out her Personal Compass notes.

A Few Questions If I May?

1. *But the whole world and especially my boss seems to be on clock time. It just seems to be a bit of a luxury to stop and think or to be able to save significantly for the future or even choose the career that you really wish to do.*

You're certainly correct that we are in a clock world and increasingly so. There always appears to be more to be done in less time. And in the global economy, the clock is 'open' 24 hours a day, seven days a week. But it doesn't mean <u>you</u> have to run your life that way. And it is certainly not a luxury. Switch from just clock thinking to compass and clock thinking and you will find your clock thinking becomes so much easier.

2. *A lot of these are pretty tough to turn around, e.g. my finances are a total mess as a result of a lot of university debt.*

They may well be. Part of the challenge is that nobody gives us any guidance to set our compass. It's unlikely to be done at school or at college. And possibly it's not something your parents will have reviewed with you, so we continue to work with clock time. We have a course to be paid for: let's borrow the money. We're very busy: let's stop going to the gym … The only problem is that compass issues have to be addressed some time: the sooner we action them the better. So yes, you are right – some of these are tough to turn around, but it can be done. Slowly but surely and you will feel great once you are making progress.

3. *What if you and your partner disagree over the direction of your compass?*

Sounds as if you have a healthy relationship! Because you are different, you will have differences. You may have strong views which mean you do not agree on how to school your children. Or whether to save or not. Or politics or how often housework should be done or … And even if you do agree on something you might change your mind. That's a benefit of the compass: it gives you an intelligent forum for discussion. It allows you both to air your thoughts, worries and dreams well before they become critical so that they can be discussed and supported.

And Now Back To You

1. **There's clock time:** this is the time which is generally important and urgent: we are up against the clock and up against our schedule. Nothing wrong with this time of course: we do all need to be fast, flexible and responsive. But if we are always in this time we will find that things just get faster and faster and tougher and tougher until eventually …

2. **And there is compass time:** we appreciate another kind of time: that which is important and investing. Ironically it doesn't always seem so relevant because it is not urgent. Our career is not urgent, our health is not urgent, our relationships are not urgent. Until they are going wrong, at which point it is often too late or certainly much, much more difficult to repair, fix or address.

3. **There are six points on your Personal Compass:** each of these will take you in a different direction, each will have huge implications for the life you lead. Choose carefully ...

4. **Career:** what do you really, really want to do? What are you best at? What feels less and less like a job, but something which is fundamentally who you are? You can get good at it and consequently you can earn well.

5. **Wellness:** how can you get to a stage where you have natural energy, focus and an inclination to act?

6. **Finance:** how do you get it sorted to give yourself freedom? Understand that it is not the real motivator.

7. **Relationships:** alongside career, the other real cause of happiness in your life. But like any other compass point it needs attention.

8. **Fun:** think beyond money, alcohol and special events. How could it be more part of the day-to-day?

9. **Contribution:** giving back means you'll grow too.

10. **Check the compass:** once a month review each compass point.

11. **Share the compass:** with those with whom you are sharing the journey.

12. **Live the compass:** transfer identified actions to your Master List.

YOU, ONLY BETTER • **SECTION 4** $\longrightarrow$

HOW TO
BOOST YOUR
PRODUCTIVITY

You, Only Better

You've been working on your career; that was Chapter 1. You've made excellent progress on boosting your energy; that was Chapter 2. You're now working on your Personal Compass – Chapter 3 of course. As a result of those studied reflections you are identifying that there are things to be done to create an even better version of you: perhaps take out an ISA to start saving some money, perhaps a conversation is needed with your boss about how you are viewed in the team, maybe you have simply committed to taking more walks. All well and good, but of course we cannot forget all the things which never go away, such as children to be picked up from nursery, bills to be paid and e-mails to be answered.

How do you get things done?

No, how exactly do you get the right things done?

NOW WITH ADDED PRIVACY SETTINGS

WARNING CONTENTS MAY DAMAGE CAREER AND CAUSE LOSS OF FRIENDSHIP IF USED UNDER INFLUENCE OF ALCOHOL

Set Your Compass

Before we answer that question fully, let's just return to the Personal Compass. This of course we worked on in the last chapter: we reflected on the six compass points of (1) career (2) wellness (3) personal finance (4) relationships (5) fun and (6) contribution. And the reason for setting your compass was to do something many people never quite get around to: deciding what is important in your life. Because few would disagree that everything must stem from knowing that. Issues such as work/life balance cannot be resolved without knowing what is important. Being able to effectively prioritise, not just at home or at work but also home vs. work, can only be done when we know what is important. And most critically getting the right things done will never happen without knowing what is truly important: without knowing what *are* the right things.

Manage From a Master List

But back to that question: once you know what is important as a result of careful work with your Personal Compass, how do you get it to actually happen? Here's the really good news: it's actually remarkably straightforward but you will need to let go of some poor habits: **you need to manage your life from your Master List**. *Not a 'to do' list, not who's shouting loudest or longest, not what is first up in your in-box on your phone*. **No, your Master List.**

A Master List is an incredible tool: *it is one list in one place of everything you have to do and want to do – both home and work – in one place*. If you like, it is your flight-deck: it gives you a complete overview of everything which needs attention. Imagine on your flight to Spain you notice that the pilot every so often wanders the entire length of the plane to look out of the back window to see what is happening: it'd be crazy. We expect our pilot to have all the data he or she needs in one place so that they can make all the necessary decisions and adjustments necessary for a great and safe journey. Same for you: too often we simply don't have the ability to make the right decision as we don't have the right data conveniently in one place. That's the Master List. The Personal Compass is the strategic route planning tool; the Master List is the tactical implementation of that.

FEW ON PLANET EARTH
REALISED THAT ALIENS
FROM FAR GALAXIES
HAD SEEDED PLANET EARTH
WITH THE TERRIBLE
VIRUS KNOWN AS 'E-MAIL'

ONCE BROADBAND
CONNECTIONS WERE
COMPLETE IN TIBET,
EARTH WOULD

GRIND TO A HALT

AND THE JEWEL OF
THE UNIVERSE

WOULD BE THEIRS...

So, before continuing with some details of the Master List, let's just ditch some poor practices:

Poor Practice 1: the 'to do' list. Oh yes, it's a perennial favourite. The 'to do' list is at best efficient, i.e. it gets stuff done. But it is not necessarily good at getting the <u>right</u> stuff done, nor the long-term stuff, nor more personal stuff. In fact at times it can be worse than that: it becomes so absorbing, the self-congratulatory 'tick' of quick-fix achievement becomes so important, that we really do lose sight of what is vital. No, that won't help us get the right things done. At best it will keep us in the swamp of what is urgent and often – truth be told – what is trivial.

Poor Practice 2: the 'BlackBerry fool'. This is the person for whom the Holy Grail is to keep their in-box down to a minimum so they are constantly checking it. The problem is, of course, that the nature of much e-mail is that it tends to be short-term and rarely about significant personal stuff. Once again we get sucked into the here and now dealing solely with what is urgent. We lose our horizon, we lose our mountain top view, we lose our perspective.

Poor Practice 3: the 'yellow stickies'. Quick: grab another one; jot it down, stick it on the screen. Again: short-term, urgent and easy to apply but so easy to forget a critical item and difficult to prioritise. So much fun to use and we are clearly visibly busy. But let's not kid ourselves: an essential priority could easily be missed.

Poor Practice 4: a curious belief *'if it's important, it will happen'*. A philosophical view point. If only. The reality though is that if it is urgent it might get done. But much that is important does not actually get addressed.

No. if you wish to be effective there is only one way: the Master List; let's get detailed.

Using the Master List

Start with an A4 spiral notebook or whatever format you prefer and start to capture the things you need to do, want to do, both at work and at home. Use these questions as prompts to your thinking:

- *What do I have to do at work?*

- *What do I have to do at home?*

- *What do I want to do at work?*

- *What do I want to do at home?*

- *What would I do at work if only I could find the time?*

- *What would I do at home if only I could find the time?*

- *What are a few dreams and crazy thoughts both at work and home?*

The first role of the Master List is to capture anything to which you want to give attention. This means you want to consider it more. That might mean that you are actually going to do it. Or it might mean you are going to plan it or allow it to incubate for a while before deciding whether it needs further serious consideration. It is a great reliever of stress to know that it is on your list. And as you will see that means it can never be forgotten.

The second role of the Master List is to prepare any item for action. At the end of the day spend 10 minutes reviewing the Master List and identifying anything which is big, chunky and possibly daunting and break it down into small, bite-sized chunks: 45 minutes is an ideal chunk; most brains and/or diaries can cope with that.

The third role is to now decide from your Master List – that open list, that list of possibilities and wishes and dreams – what you will actually do tomorrow: you thus create your closed list, your day list.
Let's just summarise that:

1. Your Master List is a bag of everything to which you want to give attention.

2. The bag needs to be full of manageable sized items in order to make processing easy, so at the end of every day break anything big down into brain and time friendly pieces.

3. Following that 'break and break' process, now date, i.e. decide when you will do it, most critically that which you will do tomorrow of course.

4. Decide what, from your <u>open</u> Master List, will go onto your <u>closed</u> day list by ensuring that you (1) respect your compass (2) respect the busyness of your day and (3) respect your personal energy flow.

5. That's it.

Let's just add some helpful detail for your implementation.

That scanning and planning process

As you scan your Master List you will view items that are work related (*'create a PPT deck for the sales meeting'*), some which are personal (*'first round of visits for Jo's secondary schooling'*), some which are about now (*'why does the insurance direct debit seem much higher than it should be?'*) and maybe some which are concerned with five years' time (*'that start-up which I keep dreaming about...'*).The purpose of this second part of the ML review is to decide what you will work on tomorrow and you do that by ensuring all aspects of your compass are represented: work hard to not let a day go by without each compass point getting some attention. You will also need to bear in mind: what kind of a day do I have tomorrow? Plenty of work time or back-to-back meetings? The former will indicate a generous closed/day list, the latter a more restricted one.

Finally take your Master List and group it by similar tasks and also flex it by your best working times, i.e. if you are a morning person then when you arrive at your desk at 8 am you might avoid even checking e-mail until you have done an hour's writing on your strategy documents.

FORTUNATELY
HE
KNEW
THAT
A LITTLE KNOWN
4TH LAW OF ROBOTICS (QV. ISAAC ASIMOV)
WAS
THAT

06:23

'GIVEN ANY OPPORTUNITY
AN ALARM CLOCK
WILL LIE TO
HIS/HER
OWNER'

Maintaining the Master List

What feeds the ML?

Firstly the Personal Compass of course. Once a month you check each compass point and consider what needs to be done. This is not only a check, it is also a balance: each compass point respecting the other.

Secondly anything which comes to mind: jot it down for focused consideration at the end of the day.

Thirdly use the time period change of the week, quarter and year to prompt your thinking, i.e. at the end of the week, ask: what do I need to consider for next week? At the end of the quarter, ask: what do I need to anticipate for next quarter? And at the end of the year, ask: what needs vital consideration next year?

Rapid Review of Staying Productive in a World Gone Mad

You are poised to be super productive. You know what is important to you both at work and at home. You are able to keep careful reflective balance across all points of your compass. Now the only real challenge is your state of mind and the world of distractions! And neither should be underestimated.

Staying Focused, Having a Plan and Keeping Distraction at Bay

Focus

Once you know what you need to focus on, then focus is a state of mind: the ability to concentrate, maintain clarity and have enthusiasm for the task in hand. And how do you do that? Chapter 2, of course: energy. The areas of that chapter which are particularly critical are meditation or taking time out, sleep and care with food. Meditation is self-evident: a busy, distracted and worried mind finds it very difficult to concentrate. Thus regularly clear the head. Sleep too is clear: a head which keeps nodding forward in its desperation for some rest is unlikely to do a great job. Diet maybe needs a word or two: be careful with the stimulants which mess with your mood: too much of anything such as coffee or sugar can cause you to find it difficult to stay sharp.

Have a plan

This is your closed list, your day list. It contains a flow during the day which has been optimised for the commitments you already have, for the things you need to achieve and how and when you work best.

Distraction

You must now of course keep distractions at bay, as they are many:

Potential Distraction 1: E-mail. What I'm going to suggest with e-mail is true of any of the digital DISTRACTORS: Twitter, Facebook etc. The biggest breakthrough in behaviour is to not be 'on-line' all of the time. Stop the flow, disconnect from the torrent and get on with some work. How long you can ignore the flow will depend upon your job. But let's suggest you work in 45-minute chunks and then review. Thus work for 45 minutes, now review all input: mail, texts, paper, tweets, etc. etc., your goal being to get all the receptors of these back to zero or 'in-box zero'. This is done by ensuring every piece of digital flotsam and jetsam is considered in one of three ways. Firstly should it be deleted? If so: delete it. Secondly should it be filed? If so, file it. Thirdly, should it be creating an action? If so, it of course goes on to your Master List for daily consideration and processing.

Potential Distraction 2: People. People? A distraction? Sure: you love them of course, but they can very easily ensure you never really get done what needs to get done.

Let's take two simple cases:

Case 1: Members of your team keep disturbing you. Your 'door' – whether or not it is real – is always open. And of course it seemed like a good policy initially: any question they have they can come to you and you can resolve it. The dilemma is you have a constant flow of interrupts and never get any thinking time. You are also becoming suspicious that instead of sorting anything out for themselves, it's just easier for them to come straight to you. Here's how you sort it. At a team meeting you explain to the team that your 'door' will be closed at certain times. That when people come to you with a query, you expect a first pass solution to the question. As a result of this new approach, interrupts have plummeted, you get more undisturbed work time and the team are being trained in how to take more responsibility.

Case 2: Your boss comes to you and asks you to take on an extra piece of work but not drop any of your current workload. You certainly don't want to seem difficult – after all business is tough and jobs are vulnerable. However you do have a new baby at home and getting home on time is critical. And you are perfectly aware from past experience that the more you take on, the more you end up doing. Here's how you sort it: you arrange a private conversation with your boss and stress how much you appreciate the extra responsibility, however you do want to do an excellent job, therefore how and what can you re-schedule to help you do a great job on an increasing workload?

Potential Distraction 3: Meetings. Poorly run meetings are of course an example of people at their worst: lateness, lack of clarity and an inability to agree actions. Make a decision to do your utmost to get a meeting to start and finish on time, to be clear on its objective and to conclude with clear, measurable actions. But how on earth is that done? Read about assertiveness below.

Potential Distraction 4: Poor Systems. When you consider what you do on a daily basis, you might split things into Vital Few (e.g. coaching some of your team, preparing a pitch for the new client or making decisions on new product launches). *Vital few tend to have a big impact, a big return on the time investment.* And Trivial Many (getting expenses done, coping

IT HIT HER

LIKE A
BOLT OF
ELECTRICITY

WHY WOULD
SHE LET A JERK
OF A BOSS SPOIL
HER DAY?

SHE
HAD
DISCOVERED
THAT
THE
SHOWER
WAS
THE
LAST
PLACE
ON
PLANET
EARTH
THAT
SHE
COULD
THINK

IT WAS AFTER ALL INPENETRABLE TO
TEXTS, E-MAILS, ALARM CALLS, TODDLERS,
CONTINUOUS ROLLING ARMAGEDDON NEWS,
CONFERENCE CALLS, SPAM, DOUGHNUTS,
MISSIVES FROM HER BOSS
SHE LOVED IT

with lots of e-mail or sorting out a problem caused by a quality issue). Trivial many tend to be time consuming and have a low return on the time invested. BUT they need to be done. How do we reconcile this? Look for a system that makes it easy. Let's take a look at two:

System 1: for expenses. Keep a large brown paper envelope for all receipts and a spiral reporter's notebook. Date, number and explain the receipt, e.g. receipt October 34, Pete's Pizza, 42.26. In your spiral notebook make that entry. Once a week (not once a month) reconcile your expenses and submit them promptly and easily once a month. Note that the system makes it easy to invest small, not arduous, chunks of time up front to get the job done rather than onerous larger chunks of time later on.

System 2: ensuring investment activities such as coaching Allen. Sit down and book them up to one year in advance. They will happen.

Assertiveness

The approach you are taking in many of the cases above is to be assertive. You are respecting your rights and you are respecting the rights of the other person. If you simply worry only about your own rights and ignore those of the other person then you are in danger of being aggressive. If you do not respect your own rights then you are of course being passive. Let's take the more specific example of the meeting.

The meeting is meant to be running from 0900 to 1000. By 0905 only you and the facilitator and two of the four who should be attending are present. Start. To delay is not respecting those who got there on time and is rewarding the behaviour of those who are late. Stop people who are going off topic: they are not respecting the time of other people.

Assertiveness is a very powerful method of ensuring that the right things get done.

Kaizen

Kaizen is a Japanese word and it means constant, never-ending improvement. In an ever more demanding world, improve your productivity systems by plan-do-review. Plan it: what do we need to anticipate? Do it: work at it hard and smart. And then review it: what did we learn? What needs to be done differently? Through the use of kaizen you will consistently become more productive.

Josh and Liza

To anyone looking in, their life seemed wonderful. Nice house, great jobs, cool cars and two energetic children. And it was – sort of. But for Josh and Liza, the dream was palling. Both had been graduate high performers, both had become high earners, both wanted children and to climb the ladder of their respective careers.

But the cracks were now starting to appear: in a nutshell, life was a frantic run through the week which was total chaos. Just when Josh and Liza felt they might get a rest it was the weekend and children wanted their attention. Both of their once very secure jobs were now under a huge amount of pressure and so both felt obliged to be working 24/7. Salaries had been frozen for three years but of course their personal cost base was ever increasing. Their children were getting to an age where clubs, trips, events and holidays were taking significant amounts of money. And a decade of good times had not prepared them for a period of austerity. Food shopping had never had a budget, pretty well everything went on a credit card and it was assumed that the value of the house and the vague notion of a pension would sort everything out at some date in the future.

Bump. That's how they landed on Friday night when Josh was made redundant with just the statutory minimum for redundancy. The weekend was hell: recriminations on both sides. Ifs, buts and what might have beens … Blame of employers and governments. 'What ifs' of children and previous expensive holidays and credit card bills and falling pension stock …

Monday, Josh woke up and said that by the time his wife was back at the end of the day he'd have a plan. He kissed and waved them all off, grabbed his gym kit and went for a run. He made some coffee, went upstairs and dug out some old notes from a year ago. Compass or something, here it was ... yeah, that was right. Some useful stuff here: had actually thought it pretty useful on the course at the time but ... well ... whatever – he was going to get it to work now. OK. He grabbed one of the many notebooks on his desk, put on an old Bowie playlist he had created ... haha ... heroes indeed ... and dived in. Might as well start with finance he thought ...

Three hours later he came up for air. He was feeling better already. He had three A4 pages of actions and one page of points to discuss with Liza.

He grabbed a blanket, threw it around himself and went to meditate in the sunny part of the living room. One action was to start looking after himself again: just limiting booze would get their finances into a better state.

And then soup and another hour.

Later that evening he and Liza had one of the deepest conversations they had had for a long time. They agreed that everything was going to be alright. That there was plenty they could do. That the whole thing had broken because it was due to break. They needed to build a lifestyle which was more sustainable and sustaining. And that was down to them.

START IT TODAY

PROCRASTINATION
IS
SO
'YESTERDAY'

A Few Questions If I May?

1. I may be organised, but I still need more time.

There are two issues here. One is that few people realise how much poor organisation, poor systems and the allowing of distraction into their lives cost in terms of time (and of course by implication stress and often money too). Decide to get organised and the return will follow. Issue two is of course that there are some people who are trying or are being asked to do too much. In which case a conversation – an assertive conversation – needs to be had.

2. I'd love to execute the batch process you describe but I don't think my boss would put up with that.

Hopefully your boss wants you to hit your objectives. Explain to him or her that that is your goal too. Ask him to give you a trial couple of weeks where you do change a few working practices for the longer term goal of becoming more productive. It seems as if that is something no reasonable boss could refuse. Ahhh: well that's a bigger issue for you then!

3. But what about some spontaneity?

Yes, it perhaps does feel like that: structure, organisation and systems. Where's the fun, the spontaneity? Here's the key: with structure, organisation and systems there is more time with more fun. You will feel – and actually be – freer than you have ever been before. You do not need to work in the evening, you do not need to answer your work e-mail on holiday ... none of this is the antithesis of spontaneity: it encourages it.

And Now Back To You

1. Once a month, **set your compass**, i.e. regularly give proper consideration to all aspects of your life: career, wellness, personal finance, relationships, fun and contribution.

2. Each compass point will need regular attention: such **action points are captured on your Master List.**

3. By considering all compass points simultaneously you will ensure **work/life balance.**

4. At the end of each day, **review your Master List.**

5. Firstly **break down any larger items** into chunks which are both time and brain friendly, i.e. they feel easily achievable. Aim for pieces of work which can be done in about 45 minutes.

6. Secondly choose **which specific items** you will give attention to the following day. Bearing in mind any prior commitments such as meetings which you already have and when you work best, schedule your next day list, which is your closed list.

7. You have now managed the primary mechanic of **getting the right things done.** It is now critical that you **look after your state** or how you are, which is primarily about meditation, sleep and quality balanced nutrition. If you are in a good state you will be able to work not just efficiently (getting things done) but also effectively (getting the right things done).

8. The secondary mechanic is to **now schedule what needs to be done** from your closed list around your meetings and whilst respecting your daily energy flow.

9. The potential wrecker of your productivity, of your getting things done, is the **tidal wave of distractors** of which there are many: people interrupts, mail, poor systems, poorly run meetings. We discussed ways of managing such distraction through batch processing, systems and assertiveness.

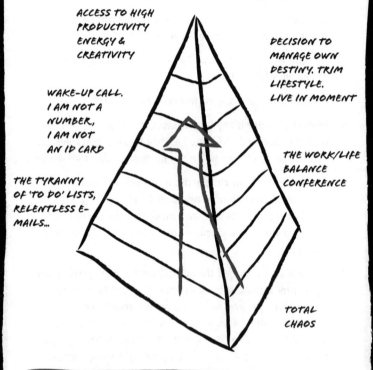

SYNCHRONISATION
OF WORK PASSION
AND LIFE
ENHANCING PLANET
SAVING STUFF

ACCESS TO HIGH
PRODUCTIVITY
ENERGY &
CREATIVITY

DECISION TO
MANAGE OWN
DESTINY. TRIM
LIFESTYLE.
LIVE IN MOMENT

WAKE-UP CALL.
I AM NOT A
NUMBER,
I AM NOT
AN ID CARD

THE WORK/LIFE
BALANCE
CONFERENCE

THE TYRANNY
OF 'TO DO' LISTS,
RELENTLESS E-
MAILS...

TOTAL
CHAOS

THE
PYRAMID
OF
PRODUCTIVITY

YOU, ONLY BETTER • SECTION 5 ⟶

MANAGE
YOUR
THINKING.
MAKE GREAT
DECISIONS.
GET IT TO
HAPPEN.

It's our most powerful asset: it can get us out of any problem or dilemma. It can change sad to happy and back to sad. It can fill time. It can get fed up with time. It's the route to decisions, from who to marry to what business to start up. It can cause a headache, it can drive a conversation for hours and it can suggest when enough is enough.

Thinking, our greatest **hidden** asset. Almost anything else which makes us smart is obvious: our eyes and ears and nose are there all the time. Our dexterity is at the end of our arm. But our thinking: it's hidden away, mysteriously. And how do we get it to work at its best? More sleep? Or more coffee? Or go sit on a beach and look at the sunrise?

Quite: man's greatest asset but surely one of the ones we 'use' least well on a day-to-day basis. Let's change that.

Why Is Thinking So Important?

It's perhaps worth considering this 'daft' question. With thinking you have options. When you don't think you are no more than a machine; once you have options you can take your life any place you please. As you'll see, many of the problems you perhaps think (there we go, you see) you have are merely problems of thinking: thus.

Jill is a very senior and a well-paid analyst at one of the larger oil companies. She's been in the job for 19 years and its attractions are fading, although the salary and security are of course well understood and appreciated. Recently she took up watercolours, mainly as a hobby, but has actually discovered she is very good at it and can sell a framed version of one of her paintings for around £300. Not bad, but not enough to retire on which she would love to do. Her thinking revolves around the powerful word 'or': should she stay with her current company or should she take the plunge and develop her painting skills but with the risk of not earning enough money? Her thinking was leading her astray: it doesn't need to be 'or', it could be 'and'.

Confused?

But hang on: surely we cannot stop thinking! Surely we think all the time. I think it's going to rain, I think 'I'll get the bus'. It's what we do ... think. You are right of course. It's partly a use of language as well. So without getting too complicated perhaps we can agree that we do of course think all the time, but this chapter is addressing that 'purposeful', 'proactive' thinking rather than just the day-to-day 'whirrings' of the human mind.

How Does 'Thinking' Work?

Let's introduce a simple model: reptile brain and higher/human brain. Reptile brain is the brain from early in our evolution of course, and it's brilliant: it saves us from crazy accidents every day with its fast 'impulsive' response. Of course that amazing ability can be frustrating: reptile brain is pattern seeking and likes to do things the way it always does things: same route to work each morning, listen to the same things on the radio, same views, same beliefs ... Our goal is to appreciate reptile brain but to get human/higher brain to engage as often as is possible as it is an essential route to being the best version of ourselves. Our goal is to stop ourselves getting dulled and surviving on auto cue and coffee.

BREWING TIME?
THE FIRST BIG
DECISION OF THE DAY

What Dulls Us? What Stops Our Best Thinking?

To be honest: a whole range of things:

Busyness: when we get busy, the only way we can survive, the only way we can get through the day is to rely on reptile brain. Thus we can very quickly get a one-dimensional view of the world: meetings, e-mail, targets to be hit, all with their commensurate problems. Reptile, survival brain says 'get through the meeting': it is less concerned with whether it is a great meeting. Reptile, survival brain says 'hit the target': it is less concerned about whether it was a profitable deal.

Stress: busyness of course tends to lead to stress and stress pushes us into the famous 'fight or flight' model where our choices are often really limited or at the very least feel limited, and often our worst behaviours of avoidance or aggression come to the fore. Higher brain, once engaged, allows a whole spectrum, a whole span of options.

Fatigue: deep tiredness causes us to want to stop, to want to give up. Only reptile brain will continue to fight the cause: it will get us to continue to drive up the motorway late at night when that appears to be the sole goal. There is a bigger goal, of course, and that is to do that drive safely. Reptile brain may draw us into a risk which human/higher brain would perceive and avoid.

Fear: fear drives us once again into fight or flight with all the associated limitations. We appreciate it when we are in an emergency, but often it kicks in unnecessarily when there is no real risk at all.

Patterns: same old, same old. If we have been there before, there is a tendency to take the same old path, which is a shame as the high road or the low road might lead us to just what we are seeking.

Other people: sadly, other people often want us to stay exactly the same as then we are not threatening to them in any way at all. We do not remind them of what they, too, might do ...

Limited experience: sometimes if our experience is limited it is difficult to envisage a fresh approach.

And So How Do We Get Access to Our Best Thinking?

Our best thinking is a combination of:

Firstly, looking after yourself, which is of course Wellness in Chapter 2.

Coupled with, not worrying about what other people think, managing fear, accelerating our experience and being able to play with our perception. We've done plenty on wellness, but now would be the perfect time to look at how you can improve the quality of your thinking by managing the other four factors.

Boosting Your Best Thinking

Other people. Although other people can encourage and might share useful wisdom, and do sometimes have useful feedback, we must ultimately stay <u>self-referenced</u> rather than externally referenced. When we are self-referenced, it means we stick to our view, we stick to what is important to us. It does not mean we are selfish nor does it mean we ignore feedback, but it does mean we are not going to change our views simply so that we don't disturb someone else's view. Let's take a couple of examples:

Example 1. It was a great weekend and Friday night was party night as was Saturday night and Sunday was down the pub at lunch time. Sunday night your head is hurting and you generally don't feel that great. No problem: a few days off alcohol, until Thursday, you decide. On Wednesday some friends invite you down the pub; initially reluctant you finally say you'll come but you won't be drinking alcohol. And what happens once you walk in the pub? Pressure to drink. At this point you can either be self-referenced, which means you stick to what is important to you and say: *'great to see you all but I'm not drinking anything, thanks'*. That's self-referenced of course. Or you can have the drink and then another drink just to keep them happy; but regret it yourself later. That is externally referenced.

 HALF FULL

 HALF EMPTY

 TOPPED UP

 RE-SPECCED

SPILT

WASHED + DRIED

 HURLED + SMASHED

OPTIONS ARE RARELY EITHER/OR

Example 2. You've been thinking for some time about experimenting with an on-line business perhaps selling ladies' jeans made out of premium Japanese denim. You've been doing a lot of reading and surfing of the web to see what is out there. It's Saturday afternoon, your boyfriend is out and you and your notebooks and iPad are spread all over the sofa; you are planning and thinking and enjoying the possibilities of your own business. Your boyfriend returns: *'what the heck is going on?'*, he exclaims. *'All you do these days is study and talk business. I think I enjoyed the old you more when you just wanted to go shopping.'* Don't react: stay self-referenced and suggest something along the lines of: *'please don't give me a hard time on this. Support would be nice. I'll bring you up to date with what I have been doing and then maybe we can watch a film?'*

Accelerating our experience. Travel broadens the mind. True: it's one of the most dramatic examples. But it's also true that almost anything broadens the mind if the brain is receptive: discussion, a movie, watching storm clouds gather. But one thing does it quickly, any time, any place and on a budget, and that is reading. Always have a book on the go: it will dramatically broaden and deepen the nature of your thinking.

Fear. Fear causes us to close down. Understandably: it's about taking no risk, self-preservation. We will see some good strategies for dealing with fear a few paragraphs on.

Perceptional perspective. Any situation can be looked at in a number of ways. To boost your thinking, always look at a situation in the most resourceful way. For example:

Do you say to yourself *'I am not getting any interviews'* or do you tell yourself *'I need to strengthen my CV and covering letter?'*

Do you believe *'I just can't get fit'* or do you think *'I need to accept that the gym does not work for me'*, and find some method which does help?

Our Personal Operating System

The last two examples in the last paragraph (fear and perceptual perspectives) introduced us to a fascinating aspect of our thinking. We are all familiar with our phones and computers having operating systems on which the 'apps' run. It's clearly very important that the operating system is a good one and is also up to date. We too have an operating system: we have a set of beliefs, a mindset if you will, which governs how we think. As you can see, the analogy of software is a good one. And often for many of us the operating system is not a particularly useful one, nor has it been upgraded for a while. This will fundamentally stop us being the best version of ourselves as ... ready ...?

Belief (or mindset) drives behaviour drives results. Thus if you believe that you are not good enough to contribute to the team meeting, then there is a real likelihood that you will not. And if you don't then you won't get any experience of contributing so you will continue to reinforce that limiting belief: *'I'm weak at contributing to meetings'*. There are broadly two kinds of beliefs: those which help or are empowering, such as *'yes, I can increase my creativity'*. Or limiting, such as *'I am not a creative person'*. Clearly empowering beliefs support the concept of *You, Only Better*. Limiting beliefs will hold us back.

Limiting belief examples

Labels, e.g. *'I'm too old'*. There are one or two things we are perhaps not so good at when we are older. But to say (at age 30) *'I'm too old to learn a new language'* is simply not true. Or (at age 60) *'I'm too old to get fit'* is not true either.

Generalisations, e.g. *'I never get an opportunity'*. Well perhaps you have missed out on some opportunities. But have you NEVER had an opportunity in your life? Quite!

Empowering belief examples

No failure, only learning.

I can do anything. But I can't do everything.

Improving Our Thinking

So thinking is our greatest asset: understood. And our thinking can be improved by basics such as TLC and managing our personal operating system. And then it dawns on us that our thinking is like any skill: it needs practice and there are tactics we can choose to develop that practice power. Thus:

Proactive thinking

Which considers the question, **what do I need to anticipate**? Regular asking of this question will help us stay at the top of our game. Thus:

In our business, which is currently very successful, what do I need to anticipate to ensure that

- our competitors cannot begin to close in on us
- we do not get too busy to innovate
- we avoid complacency
- we do not get too big so that some people who don't like working in the larger organisation any more will be poached by a competitor?

In our personal life, what do I need to anticipate ...

- that the kids are coming up to secondary school and we really dislike the current options ... for schooling
- that I would like to slow down but I still need to be earning money?

Critical thinking

Ask the question, what do I/we need to do better?

Thus, in our business which is a small electrical store, what do we do to ensure we are not hit by the on-line businesses?

Thus, in our family life, how can we get more time together?

THE QUESTION MARK

OF YES? OR NO?

THE PARENTHESES

OF THINGS UNSPOKEN

Lateral thinking

This is the basis of creativity and is, in essence, the question: what do I need to do differently?

Thus, how can I get more contact with senior people in the organisations with which I deal? Because one thing is certain, the methods I am using now are failing.

Thinking, Decisions, Actions

Although there is of course a pleasure in 'just thinking', e.g. 'just' day dreaming, much of the time we are thinking to a purpose. How to get our household costs down, how to get out of a messy relationship without too many tears or simply which T-shirt to buy. When we think to a purpose, we are in effect intent on making a decision. Thus you have been thinking a lot about your health recently and have decided to join a gym. Excellent. One month later: have you joined the gym, yet? Er, no. You see a decision is not an action. So we realise there are three stages:

Stage 1, the thinking. We've covered plenty of ground on that.

Stage 2, the decision. We need to do a little work on that.

Stage 3, the action. Getting it to happen. Ditto.

Decisions

There are a few potential strategies to making a better decision assuming you have done the background thinking.

One is to weigh up the pros and cons, i.e. create a simple T-bar with the pros and cons on either side. Are there more pros than cons to buying a new car rather than a second hand car? To changing job rather than working your way up with your current firm? A pros and cons approach is certainly worth doing, less perhaps because it helps you form the final decision, more that it clarifies your thinking and reveals where you need to get more data or simply to think some more. It also needs to be borne in mind that, especially when we are making decisions on our own, we often know the conclusion we want and simply stack the columns to give the appearance of a more logical approach!

BOLD

SURE
IS
WASTED
ON
COFFEE

- BOLD PEOPLE
- BOLD THINKING
- BOLD ACTION
  ## NOW!

Another is to mull it over. It's amazing how 24 hours can put things in perspective. Only yesterday we were never ever going to consider speaking to him again. But now, maybe the real learning is for us, having reflected on how controlling we have become. Formally called 'incubation', it's powerful.

Yet another is to get someone else's opinion. Everybody's brain is unique, so bring another brain into play and you get another perspective. A good decision considers all of the perspectives.

Or of course to combine all three: which perhaps gives us the best overall strategy for making a decision:

FIRSTLY: do a 'pros/cons' to get clarity. Get the detail and the facts compared. And maybe if it's a straightforward or simple decision that will be enough. If not ...

SECONDLY: get another person's perspective. Of course this may be frustrating (why didn't I think of that?), irritating (if only it were that easy!) but it should ensure balance and clarity for your own views,

THIRDLY: incubate. Reflect. Leave it a while. The brain is a marvellous thing and given some time and distance can come up with the most amazing conclusions and ways forward. And then decide. Or if it is still impossible to do so, repeat the cycle until you get the best conclusion or time runs out.

Action

Do you remember this one? *A decision is not a decision until we take an action.*

- I will go to the gym
- We will increase our market share by 42%
- I'm going to write a best seller.

All easily said. They are decisions. But they are not yet actions. What is an action? An action is breaking the decision down into components which can be achieved, owned, date stamped and measured. And eventually ticked off.

Thus 'write novel' is simply too much. But how about:

- Decide core plot 1 hour, Monday evening 7 pm to 8 pm

- Outline character of main character, Wednesday 6.30 pm to 7.30 pm

- Write first 1,000 words of opening murder scenes, Saturday morning 8–10.

Suddenly the decision can become reality. But what do you say if you don't *feel* like doing the action? That's why we did so much work on personal energy back in Chapter 2. As we said at the time much time management, much decision making is not so much about a methodology approach, it's actually about the energy to make it happen.

Jean-Paul

Jean-Paul felt he was cracking up. He couldn't assemble a decent story any more and he knew time was running out. The Listings magazine – *Le Zip List* – on which he worked was putting him under pressure and if he didn't come up with something soon he'd be back where he started, 'in the lists'. Lists of best bars, worst bars, best movies, best romantic moves, best thrillers. Lists of best English phrases, best prices on Eurostar. Lists of the perfect cocktail to seduce your new girlfriends. Yep, you get the drift: Jean-Paul didn't want to be back 'in lists'. But he needed to be able to think again. Once upon a time just choosing a café and small black coffee would get the creative juices flowing. But now all he could do was stare at his iPad. Or even worse start surfing for inspiration or start responding to e-mail.

But maybe there was hope: he liked this idea that thinking was a skill. After all he could get good at a skill. As a kid he'd become brilliant at skateboarding just by relentless daily practice. And as a student working in Le Semi-Colon wine bar he learnt about, and more importantly became able to, produce cocktails. So he was proactive but it was also about lack of distraction. With both skateboarding and cocktails that had been the main thing in his life. Now. Jeez. Now. His mother, his girlfriend, his rent, his noisy neighbours, his boss, the payment on his motorbike, his smoking habit which he didn't seem to be able to crack. His novel – *La Bicyclette qui n'a pas de nom* – which was going nowhere, the leaking window into his bedroom, the cost of eating out in Paris. And his mother. Or had he mentioned that already?

OK: so here was the plan. Thinking was a skill. He needed to be able to think better for his job, in fact everything depended on that SO he was going to dedicate himself to de-cluttering and single-minded focus just as when he was a kid and a bartender. He would start producing some good stories and, in so doing, re-secure his position of being the number 1 journalist on *Le Zip List*. Then he needed to stop kidding himself and sort out all the things in his crazy life.

Sorted.

He started.

Two weeks later he produced his best two stories ever.

Three weeks later the leaking window was fixed, eating out was only for two nights a week, smoking was reducing day by day. His mother had agreed to find her own place and the relationship with his girlfriend was better than ever. *La Bicyclette qui n'a pas de nom?* Ahhh ... that was a bigger challenge.

AS HE WATCHED THE CRASHING WAVES, THE IDEAS POURED OUT ONTO HIS REPORTER'S NOTEBOOK. HE MUST GET OUT MORE.

A Few Questions If I May?

1. *Sometimes I just find it hard to really think; I just seem overloaded: any suggestions?*

I think you have answered your own question: of course the brain can think quickly and under pressure but of necessity the result is likely to be a compromise. It is far, far better to allow the brain some reflection time. If you are regularly finding yourself having to make decisions under pressure it would be good to review Chapter 4 on productivity practices again.

2. *I notice some people seem to be able to think really quickly and come up with some great ideas. How do they do that?*

They may have a bit of a genetic advantage but it's mainly down to practice. Start throwing yourself into the meetings, stop censoring your own ideas and you will find both processes cause an increase in speed of thinking, speed of contribution and the value of what you are bringing to the meeting will increase.

3. *I find some decisions are impossible: whichever way you go you can't be sure. Is there any way to have confidence about one route or the other?*

Only by 'due diligence', i.e. by ensuring you have done everything you can to make it a quality decision. But plenty of decisions are very hard – about your career, your business, your family – and they all have consequences way down the line. Put the time in up front and early on and you should feel confident you did the best you could. And finally be assured that only a few decisions are truly final. Many, many – especially if they were good quality in the first place – can be adjusted later.

And Now Back To You

1. **Thinking is possibly our most powerful asset** and certainly it is a critical one for being the best version of ourselves.

2. **There's reptile brain and higher or human brain.** The former can and will look after itself; it's the latter we need to kick start. The former is invaluable but it is our survival brain and so will engage at any opportunity.

3. **The following can thwart higher/human brain:** busyness, stress, fatigue, fear, lack of experience, a one-dimensional perception. Much of what we have discussed in *You, Only Better* can help with managing such emotions and distractors.

4. **Which introduces us to our personal operating system:** belief/mindset drives behaviour drives results. Our 'software' will dictate our actions. But we can edit that software of course.

5. **There are limiting beliefs,** e.g. I will never get promotion.

6. **And there are empowering beliefs,** e.g. I could start networking more which would ensure my skills are more apparent to senior people in the organisation.

7. **We can improve our thinking by practising it:** it is simply a skill. Practice does make perfect. Or at least pretty damn good.

8. **There is proactive thinking,** or what do I need to anticipate?

9. **And critical thinking,** or what do I need to do better?

10. **And lateral thinking,** or what do I need to do differently?

11. We are often thinking **to reach a decision** and to take an action.

12. **There are three good ways to boost our decision-making ability:** T-bar, incubation and the views of another.

13. **There are three good ways to ensure action:** make it small and easy, give it an owner and give it a date stamp.

14. **Decisions are often not at all easy.** But delaying the decision or making an interim decision often just makes things worse. Making a really good decision is often a platform for an improved one at a later stage. Thus do not look for perfection in decision making.

YOU, ONLY BETTER • SECTION 6 ⟶

HOW TO BE
BRILLIANTLY
CREATIVE

If you are reading this book in chapter sequence you'll be noticing a steady, building, cumulative sequence of ideas and skills. To support your career goals you need energy. You tend to have more energy when you have clarity of your compass. Of course you can only make your compass happen if you are able to focus, think things through and turn thoughts into decisions and actions. And so on. On your quest to be the best version of yourself, where to from here, though? **Where to from here?** How about if you make a leap, a radical change and boldly think, 'wouldn't it be nice if I could *solve any problem I have or might ever have, be it career or financial or parenting or ...'*

That's what we are going to do now ... **Really?** Yes, really. Read on ...

In the last chapter where we were reviewing thinking, decisions and actions, we particularly isolated proactive thinking (or what do I need to anticipate?) and critical thinking (or what do I need to do better?) and lateral thinking (or what do I need to do differently?). And you will remember that we promised to come back to this latter topic because it is so crucial in *You, Only Better*.

Lateral thinking is the basis of creativity. But what is creativity, or, perhaps more helpfully, what is creativity for us? Creativity for us is identifying a fresh useful solution that we hadn't considered or even thought possible before: thus as in our earlier example, instead of thinking whether you should change your current job OR leave and concentrate on your art work maybe you could think about reducing your main job to four days a week AND do your art on the fifth day.

Life is tricky. Life is changing quickly. Who knows what the job market will be like in five years' time? Who knows how your two children will turn out in their teens? Is it possible for you to make enough money to retire much earlier? The answers to such questions, the best most resourceful answers to such questions, come from being creative.

Creativity is crucial. Who doesn't constantly need fresh solutions to bringing up teenagers, solving money dilemmas, resolving challenges with neighbours and deciding quickly which dress to wear to your son's graduation? The logical, linear approach of proactive and critical thinking sometimes reaches an impasse and that's when we need the power of creativity, of fresh thinking, of lateral thinking.

But – and it's a big but – although many people do believe that if they persevere they could become better at proactive thinking or juggling or making pancakes, so many are sure, absolutely sure, that they are simply 'not creative'.

HE
WAS
NOW
THINKING
OUTSIDE SO MANY BOXES

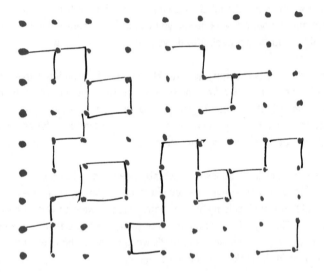

HE REALISED HE WAS
ACTUALLY
PLAYING
BATTLESHIPS

The goal of this chapter is therefore simple:

1. Firstly to give you an overall strategy (7 steps) for being more creative.

2. Secondly to give you some examples of such steps in action.

3. Thirdly to give you some tasks to continue to boost your creativity.

To work, then.

7 Principles of Creativity

Read it and think of it as a mantra or *'a simple set of instructions capable of causing transformation'*. We'll clarify it all in a moment.

1. I am creative

2. I work very hard at my creativity and accept no excuses

3. I experiment

4. I seek no approval

5. I am searching for my voice

6. I find time to be creative

7. Today is always the day.

Let's clarify the above steps ...

Step 1: I am creative. You'll remember what we did on empowering beliefs and limiting beliefs? The first place to start with boosting your creativity is to realise you are creative. We are all creative, it's just that we get dulled, we lose our self-confidence, we see our learning as mistakes and hardest of all we typically see the end results – the 'best bits' – of other people's creativity. The latter in particular can be very daunting: *'how can we ever do anything like that?'* we think. The answer is firstly to remember it is their final evolution, their final iteration: we didn't see all of their dreadful output, be it writing or art or tunes or software projects. And secondly, to do just as they did: believe in our self. In the search for techniques to be creative, all we need to remember is that the brain is mind-bogglingly creative. It just needs a chance. It doesn't need a technique. It needs opportunity. Step 1 is to realise you can be and are creative so long as you bear in mind the mantra *'I am creative'*. Of course, as with any empowering belief it can only be the start: thinking about it is not enough. It is just the support system for step 2:

Step 2: I work very hard at my creativity and accept no excuses.
To realise and to release that creativity you'll need to dig deep, you have to practise and you have to get used to the failures along the way because creating is just a skill. Yes. There I've said it. It seems so exotic, it seems to belong to the realm of musicians and writers and painters and architects and celebrity chefs. But not to 'little old me'. Yes it does and let's make it absolutely clear: it's just a skill. So: the more you try it, the better you can get. Get used to accepting no excuses: yes there is time if you make time, no you do not need a new iPad, OK you could have talked more in the pitch. Yes, it's challenging, yes somebody laughed, no you didn't get the grant this time. The more you exercise those synaptic pathways, the more you allow them to knit and take different routes, the more you will get the sparks of something fresh. Thus the second part of our mantra is crucial: *'I work very hard at my creativity and accept no excuses'*. Which neatly brings us to:

Step 3: I experiment. We are willing to try a fresh approach with our toddler's feeding routines, with our clients and their delayed payments, with our manuscript submissions and the depressing rejections. With experimentation comes the opportunity of a breakthrough. Same old often simply leads to same old. Fresh leads to fresh which maybe leads to amazing breakthrough. Sure, it leads to some rubbish along the way. We experiment by picking a page of a book at random to inspire us, by using a pencil rather than our computer to create our logo for our new home nappy service, by going to work in the park rather than the library, by only allowing ourselves five minutes to come up with an idea rather than 60 minutes. Mantra 3: I experiment. Of course, once we start experimenting we must be willing to remember that:

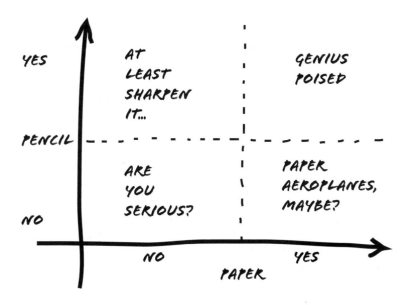

YES

PENCIL

NO

AT LEAST SHARPEN IT...

GENIUS POISED

ARE YOU SERIOUS?

PAPER AEROPLANES, MAYBE?

NO

YES

PAPER

117

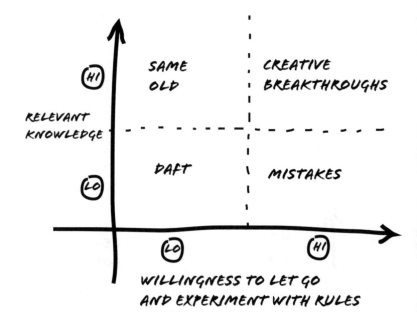

SAME OLD

CREATIVE BREAKTHROUGHS

RELEVANT KNOWLEDGE

DAFT

MISTAKES

HI

LO

LO

HI

WILLINGNESS TO LET GO AND EXPERIMENT WITH RULES

Step 4: I seek no approval. Because you simply won't get it. 'They' will see intermediary ideas for your business as daft, or time wasting or crazy, not realising that they are steps to something amazing. When aiming to boost your creativity you cannot afford to want to be loved all of the time. Our partner may initially be wary – even angry – when you suggest something radical for the education of our children. Hang on in there and use the five As of great relationships. Because, critically through the mantra of *'I seek no approval'*:

Step 5: I am searching for my voice. Yes you are. There is a unique way you have of doing things, of thinking things through which is yours alone. It's different to anyone else on the planet. It'll be really hard to find it because of all the wonderful voices to which you have been exposed: parents, teachers, writers and speakers amongst many others. Some of which have had deep and lasting resonance with you and you want to be that voice. But you cannot: it is not yours. If you copy that voice for the long term you will never develop your own and to do that:

Step 6: I find time to be creative. Time must be found. To juggle three balls effectively needs time, to be creative needs time. Your meditation time will certainly help and be a significant part of the process. Start building on that and scheduling thinking and creative times. Isolate a challenge and think about different approaches to that challenge. You work on your cooking, you work on your football, you work on your creativity. So never 'tomorrow', never 'when I have some time', never 'on vacation'. In fact ....

Step 7: Today is always the day. I will make creativity part of my life. Every day there are hundreds of opportunities to be creative. How could I get this meeting back on track? How could we save money when shopping? How could I get my boss to respect me more?

Let's see these principles in action.

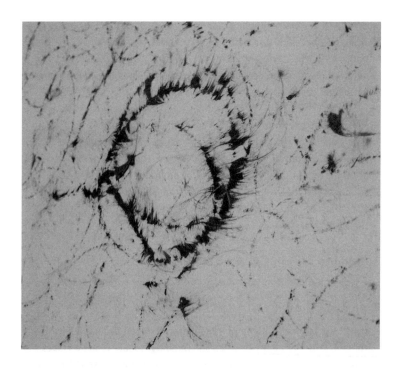

Scenarios

Scenario 1: I need more clients for my window-cleaning business

'I'm always struggling. I know we do a good job. I know we are great value. I know people need window cleaners. But I can't connect us to where the business is.'

Principle 6: I find time to be creative. Stop running around, start thinking. Start thinking reflectively. Look for patterns in your business. OK, the card drops don't work. Or maybe they don't work enough but they do work in some areas. Slow down, examine your successes and capitalise on those.

Scenario 2: I need a better relationship with my teenage daughter

'She and I are always arguing. She sees me – her mother – as out of date and controlling and trying to stop all the fun in her life. I realise that a lot of the current problems have come about because in the past I have felt guilty about not spending enough time with her and have been letting her get away with rudeness and breaking house rules.'

Principle 4: I seek no approval. To get the creative breakthrough you seek sometimes you need to defer immediate approval. You need to have a conversation with somebody which is tricky. Or you need to close down a part of a business which is not profitable for the long-term good of the rest of the business. As you think about how you can re-build this relationship, stop seeking approval. Be respectful, listen and ask that the same is done of you. Remain loving.

Scenario 3: A better plot for my novel

'My plots are not good enough. I know that. Some professional advice for which I paid told me that and the evening class I attend tells me that.'

Principle 2: I am searching for my voice. It's good general advice that to be a writer you must be a reader. The only trouble is there comes a time when you need to let go of all of that reading and start to write for yourself, not try and copy the stories of others. Stop reading for a while and start writing a lot. Truly, a lot. Your voice will appear. And when your voice appears, your ideas will appear: the plots will no longer seem like poor photocopies but fresher, imaginative and most importantly unique.

Scenario 4: I need to de-clutter my life

'My life is clutter. Physical clutter: there is hardly a surface in my flat which isn't covered in paper, books, makeup, receipts and stuff. My diary is full of things I didn't do. And my mind is spinning with worries and concerns.'

Principle 1: I am creative. You can crack this. You can sort this. Maybe you need to take a different approach and resolve your finances so that you could afford a couple of hours help from professional de-clutterers. Maybe you need to say to yourself 'I will do 15 minutes per day – just 15 minutes a day – until it is sorted even if it takes me three months'. Maybe you just need to create one clear surface to prove to yourself that you can break the patterns. The more you talk about the chaos, the more it becomes permanent and real. The key is to realise that you are creative and there is a way around this problem.

Scenario 5: Giving up smoking

'I have tried to give up smoking every January for the last six years. Every New Year's Day is hell. I drink coffee until it is coming out of my ears to try and compensate. Patches everywhere. Grumpiness for everybody. I normally last two weeks.'

Principle 3: I experiment. You mentioned it yourself, you've essentially done the same thing for six years running. You probably expect it to fail. Maybe you almost feel 'released' when it fails. Try something different – experiment. How about if you don't try and give up smoking but you do get super healthy? Walking a significant distance every day, eating loads of fresh fruit and vegetables, going to a yoga class. And perhaps your new super healthy you will simply not want so many cigarettes to get through the day. Worth a try.

Scenario 6: Getting a new job

'I have been talking for so long to so many people about getting a new job but I never do anything. Work always returns to being "OK" and I simple don't have the energy for the interviews, the endless chasing of recruitment consultants.'

Principle 7: Not tomorrow, today. You've been talking about it for over 18 months. Now is the time to start doing something about it. Make one phone call. Book one appointment. Get out there. Get some momentum. Above all, stop believing your own 'story' that you 'never do anything'.

Tasks

Consider the following simple tasks as ways of boosting your creativity on a day-to-day basis.

1. **Do something different:** read a different author, cook a different kind of meal, spend the evening in a different kind of way, listen to somebody's view that you might normally reject out of hand. Walk instead of taking the Tube, have noodles instead of rice. Get up early on Saturday rather than have a lie in.

2. **Do something differently:** make your Bolognese sauce rather than using a bottled one. Spend the weekend without TV. Spend an evening without e-mail. Listen rather than pretend to listen. Be positive whatever. Of course you don't necessarily want to do it: your body craves comfort and patterns. But if you can let go of comfort for a while then maybe you can break a pattern and as you break a pattern, maybe there is the breakthrough.

3. **Persevere a lot longer than you might usually:** do not allow yourself another coffee until those 1,000 words have been written. Turn around in the pool and do another length even if it takes you 20 minutes. Walk down another street looking for suitable properties. Setting a goal can work wonderfully. Rather than ideas for finding a cheap summer holiday, we need ten really good ideas for cheap summer holidays.

1/2 FULL?   1/2 EMPTY?

THAT'S NOT THE ISSUE...

WHETHER OR NOT
YOU ARE STAYING
HYDRATED
IS THE ISSUE...

(a) *Turn the mistake into something useful.* The soup is far too chilli hot. Dilute it and add more and then turn it into an interesting curry sauce. The life drawing isn't a life drawing. Turn it into an abstract. You don't like the hero you crafted: turn her into 'a baddy' and kill her off.

(b) *Change the scale.* Instead of lots of promotional materials just do a few and deliver them individually and by hand to the client and make them brilliant.

(c) *Look up.* Notice the beautiful architecture above the dull shops. What ideas do they give you?

(d) *Draw it.* Writing is the most common form of expression for most of us. Drawing forces a new angle. And if you are already accomplished at drawing, what about music or photography or …

(e) *Insist on speed.* Creativity sometimes somehow suggests leisure. And that might be the case. But there is nothing at all about the subject which precludes speed. So rush out those potential book titles, pencil out those house extension plans, create the slides for the presentation at incredible speed.

Arthur

Arthur had a dilemma. He loved coffee and wanted to start his very own coffee shop. Now he was a realist: he knew that this enjoyment of sitting in coffee shops and drinking perfectly made lattes was a little different to getting in at 6 am to lay out the pastries for a prompt 6.30 am opening to greet the commuters. But he reckoned he knew what he was letting himself in for. Which brought him to his second challenge (his first being was he doing the right thing? Yes!): he had no money. And just the equipment was a small fortune, even second hand. And then he'd need staff and training. And maybe he needed a partner to help him especially with the finances. And suddenly instead of that feeling of excitement in his heart and gut he just had anxiety. Ugh!

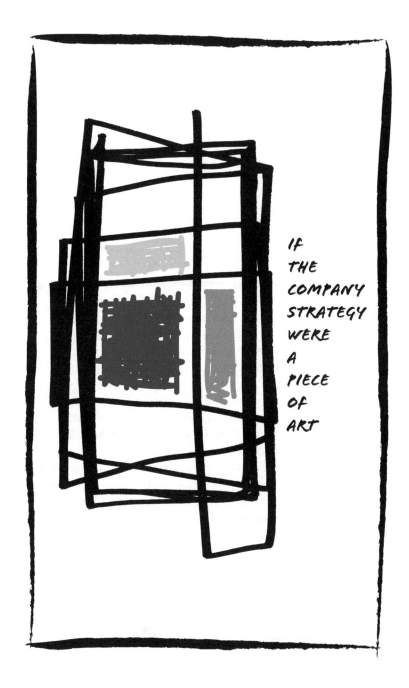

IF
THE
COMPANY
STRATEGY
WERE
A
PIECE
OF
ART

This was crazy: he knew it was what he wanted to do and he was knowledgeable about coffees and equipment. But. But he was going solve this. He pinned up the creativity mantra:

1. I am creative
2. I work very hard at my creativity and accept no excuses
3. I experiment
4. I seek no approval
5. I am searching for my voice
6. I find time
7. Today is always the day.

Next to his shaving mirror and every morning in his favoured café he worked at it. He wrote, he thought, he captured lists, he drew pictures, he struggled. The breakthrough came on day three: change the scale. Maybe he was thinking too small: could he get some venture capital? No, no, no! Another ugh: that was the last thing he wanted. Maybe he was thinking too big! How about one of those mobile espresso machines? And that meant he didn't need to give up his current job yet. He could do it weekends or maybe evenings. There was a lot to find out about. But how could he make it different? How could he brand it? More on the actual coffee bean. He had tried coffee from those mobile ones and they didn't really play much on the coffee, it was more about convenience. Maybe he could couple convenience with brilliant coffee? And they rarely had food? Just a few muffins in cellophane? How could he solve that? And maybe gluten free for the commuters? Alright: now the ideas were flowing.

A Few Questions If I May?

1. But surely some people just are more creative?

Perhaps there is a gene or genes which make it a more natural approach for some people. But you are not wholly defined by your genes and thus your creativity is only defined by the amount of work you are willing to put into the skill. Keep going back to the seven-step mantra.

2. Can any problem be solved through creativity?

It's surprising how something seemingly insurmountable from a logical or standard viewpoint can be resolved when a lateral path is taken. So, perhaps yes: if you can be creative enough any problem can be solved.

3. I've heard about techniques such as Edward de Bono's 'Six Thinking Hats' etc. Why are none of these approaches mentioned?

You are of course right that over the years numerous techniques have been expounded from *'if the problem were a body, what would the head be asking?'* to *'make more use of the red hat'*. And such techniques can have considerable value. However sometimes they simply distract from and distort your own creativity which ultimately must come from practice, self-belief and learning from feedback. So yes by all means explore books of techniques, and certainly Edward de Bono is an excellent place to start, but perhaps do not become so seduced by the tools which were designed by one person. Creativity is much more subtle than many transferable skills.

And Now Back To You

The strategy:

1. **I am creative:** believe in your capability. It is not a *'you have it or you don't'*. It is a skill that can be developed.

2. **I work very hard at my creativity and accept no excuses:** no great skill is easy. Work, work, work at it. The rewards will come.

3. **I experiment:** creativity is essentially about new pathways. Literally and figuratively in our mind.

4. **I seek no approval:** often we are only approved of when we do the same as others or we get 'success' quickly and easily. To do great things we often have to temporarily lose a person's approval.

5. **I am searching for my voice:** there is a creative version of you which is not like anybody else. Give that version a chance and it can do great things for you

6. **I find time:** give it attention, give it practice and it will blossom ...

7. **Today is always the day.**

The deliberate practice:

1. **Do something different:** choose a different path to notice, to observe, to find something different.

2. **Do something differently:** paint with oil rather than water colours. Run the meeting in the canteen rather than the board room.

3. **Persevere a lot longer than you might usually:** suggest you take a break in the negotiation. Don't give up yet: there is a way to get the deal closed to the satisfaction of both parties.

4. **Turn the mistake into something useful:** you thought the conference was a formal affair. In fact it's smart casual. Turn it into a way to get noticed and show that you're not at all concerned that you are 'different'.

5. **Change the scale:** instead of one training course a year, lots of short, fast training injections every month.

6. **Look up:** go for a walk at lunchtime. Notice the horizon and how it expands your thinking.

7. **Draw it:** or photograph it. Or act it. A different medium will create a different perspective.

8. **Do it at speed:** who knows what might be produced?

YOU, ONLY BETTER • SECTION 7 ———→

TRANSFORM YOUR LIFE: UNPLUG!

Pressure, busyness, stress. It's not fun and although it has always existed, the busyness of modern life has brought such tensions sharply into focus. We have already done some good work on reducing their impact: let's rapidly review our ideas to date:

Having a balanced Personal Compass. If you are living the life you truly want, then you'll experience less stress: there is a huge difference between working very hard on something you really want to do and something which is somebody else's goal. The **Personal Compass** is the guide to the life you seek. If you have considered it and balanced it then stress will be reduced.

Wellness. In particular, Personal Compass point 2, wellness, is about looking after yourself. If you do that then you are much more capable of handling the pressure which might be thrown at you. At the core of wellness is MEDS or meditation, exercise, diet and sleep.

The way you think. It is possible to see many potentially stressful situations in a less threatening way and the more you practise this 'perceptual positioning' approach, the easier it becomes. Is it a major argument with your partner over money or an opportunity to sort your finances once and for all? It's your choice how you look at it.

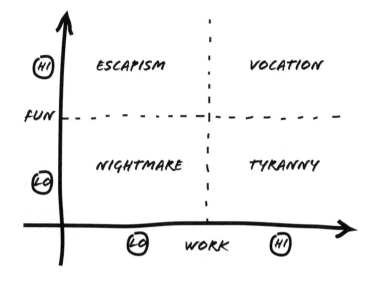

Such approaches can be really helpful. In this chapter though we will go even deeper and instead of simply working on the *mechanics* of reducing pressure and stress we will make a bigger shift which will dissolve many of the challenges by changing our fundamental thinking beyond just the tactics to a powerful potential strategy: we will go **unplugged**.

Unplugged?

Yes. Just as the rock band who have experienced all the excitement, the light shows and the big arenas want and seek desperately to get back to their roots and what is truly important to them, decide to unplug and go acoustic, so do we. We are going to unplug.

The power of unplugged is that it is more than the handy techniques we have reviewed above, it is a pragmatic and easily implementable approach, a simplification of lifestyle we can adopt (and adapt) which we can live and breathe. It becomes a part of us and is all we need to do to reduce the pressure, the demands, the overload and the stresses.

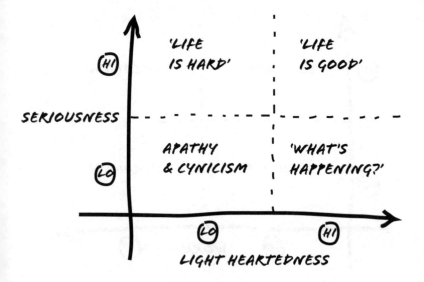

Unplugged might mean:

- Digital free evenings or part of an evening become the norm again. No e-mail, no Facebook, no screens: just conversation (even candles!) and *connecting* once again. We believe we can do it, we do not care that some of our friends see us as 'odd' for being off-line for even a whole weekend at a time. We see it as an easy and cheap way to stay sane.

- A meal cooked from scratch without any wrappers torn off: the simplest of grills with the freshest of vegetables and the easiest of clearing up. We believe it is worth the slight investment of time and perhaps some cooking utensils for a much more pleasing meal, better conversation and healthiness of food.

- Having an amazing weekend with the children without spending money. How much fun can we have without spending money? We are happy to struggle initially with our children, who keep quoting what other families are doing, as in the end they will find they are getting much more time with their parents who are themselves much more fun to be with.

- Taking the business back to its core: just two product lines brilliantly delivered consistently and without fail. We believe it is worth the transition of production lines, educating customers and re-training staff for building a business which has a sounder economic model, is more environmentally sound and is faster and more flexible to respond to market shifts.

- Spending time on what is truly important: health, a proper phone conversation with our sister ... rather than just what is urgent. We know we can do it.

- No longer trying to keep up with the latest trends all the time and accepting that doing up the house will take time but it can be done to a budget, simply and mainly through second hand goods. We know we can do it.

The essence of unplugged ...

What is the essence of unplugged? It is a return to a life of simplicity where we can truly enjoy what is most valuable and important to us.

Thus our relationships which have perhaps become far too complicated: as students we had loads of time to manage texting, e-mail, Twitter, Facebook, etc. etc. And it was good fun. Now as a parent it is simply not possible. We have deleted our Twitter and Facebook accounts and our mobile number is our simple, method of communication: it works and is all we need for our true friends.

Thus the children's schedule had become mind-boggling with far too many clubs. Two clubs have been cancelled and everybody is happier with that: you with less ferrying around the place, the children with some time to be and breathe. No, opportunities are not being lost, true opportunities are being valued in full.

Let's look at how we return to simplicity, with ten simple possible 'shifts' in approach:

Shift 1, Compass: check, balance and lighten

You are well versed in the Personal Compass: what it is, how to set it and how to balance it. There is now one final aspect to consider. As you become very conversant with your Personal Compass, as you re-set and re-balance it month on month you will start to see the synergy between each of the points and how this allows you to lighten the load. Thus the more you build a career you are enjoying, the less critical it becomes to earn lots of money to be able to pay for things to compensate for the lack of happiness in your job. The more you are able to keep your finances down to a reasonable level, the more relaxed you feel as there is less anxiety at the end of every month. The more you deliberately work on your relationships, the less you need the buzz of whole networks of adulation on Facebook. You have checked and balanced. Now you will be able to lighten.

Shift 2, Be there: now is great

Stop chasing the next experience. The next bigger experience. Enjoy the holiday in the back garden, enjoy a special birthday meal without having to go out for a meal that you cannot really afford. Simplify the children's birthday parties again as they have simply got out of hand ... Buy a car that is a few years old but will allow you to invest the 'saved money' in your start-up plans. When at work do a great job and don't keep thinking about home. And when at home, stop worrying about work. At your daughter's netball game: be there, rather than thinking about how quickly you can get away and start clearing e-mail.

Shift 3, Less is more: add one, drop one

We live in a world of opportunity and 'can do'. And so we grab those opportunities and we attempt to do them all. Yoga and Pilates classes, unlimited supplies of great TV box-sets to watch, career ladders to be climbed. Foreign holidays to be taken, holiday homes to be bought, clubs for our children to join. Houses to be made over, TV chefs to be followed, new aspects of social media to be on board with. Surfing and forums and on-line shopping. 24/7 news and bloggers. Tweeters to keep up with. We

THERE
CAN
ONLY
BE
SO
MANY

CABLES
IN
ONE
LIFE

forever add more. But the reality is 8/8/8. You need 8 hours of work, 8 hours of fun and 8 hours of sleep: the more you add the more you can damage what is actually available to you. So here is the core strategy: add one, take one. If you add your foreign language class, perhaps best to drop your Pilates class (that doesn't stop you from doing your morning Pilates yourself). If you start the new strategy review project at work, maybe it's time to wrap the separate pricing meeting into such reviews and save some significant time.

Shift 4, Simplicity: the far side of complexity. Wisdom, not just knowledge. Depth, not superficiality

Think for yourself and stop worrying about what others think.
There's a crazy treadmill it's very easy to suddenly find yourself trudging. And walking more quickly. As the busyness forces superficiality. Don't accept it. Ask tough and deep questions: what is the best education for our children? What do I want to be doing to earn a living by the time I am 45? How could we create great travel experiences for ourselves without getting into overdraft situations? Seek wisdom, not just the facts. Push for deep understanding not just a colour supplement view. But above all: think for yourself and life becomes so much easier.

Shift 5, Just say no: enough is enough. There are only so many sofas in a life-time

Accept enough. Break the addiction. Here are some addictions:

- Alcohol
- Nicotine
- Caffeine
- E-mail
- Shopping.

and there are many more of course: you must have at least one! And just as the drinker has to learn when enough is enough, and the coffee addict has to recognise that one too many espressos is causing their head to spin in a world of blistering busyness, 'unplugging' allows us to distinguish between fun and addiction, necessity and addiction, choice and addiction. Addiction can take us to a path where we no longer enjoy the process nor the result and soon we slip into dissatisfaction. Our brand new kitchen is already looking dated. It may be a lovely Mini Cooper but it's now the old model. Just say no.

Shift 6, Big rocks: proactive, not reactive

There is a famous story often told in time management/personal development circles (*a quick Google will reveal that it now seems difficult to discover the originator*). Here it is if you haven't come across it and be aware there are many variants. This is a nice simple plain 'vanilla' version:

A lecturer is trying to get across what she sees as a subtle point in time management and her students don't seem to be 'getting it', so next lecture she decides to do a demonstration and brings a large glass jar and a bucket of large 'fist-shaped' rocks. She holds up a rock and asks *'how many can we get in the jar?'* There are a few suggestions: 25, 33. The lecturer says, *'let's see …'*. As it happens she gets 31 rocks in the jar. There's space between them but she's optimised the packing so that's it. No more in the jar. She asks if it is now full and given that if she added another rock it would just fall off, she hears a resounding *'yes'* from her listeners.

'One moment' she suggests, and pulls out a bucket of pebbles from underneath the table. She takes several handfuls of the stones and feeds them down between the rocks: plenty go in. *'Is it full?'* she asks. Being a smart audience they have spotted a pattern and someone asks: *'do you have any sand?'* *'Of course'*, she replies and a few scoops of sand go in. *'Is it full?'* she asks, finally with the sand peaking and spilling onto her demonstration table? Most of the audience agree, yes, but a couple say, *'pour in your drinking water'*, which she does.

The point is, of course, that we all have a few very important things in our life: know what they are, get them in the schedule first and notice how much can be packed around them. The unplugged mentality is to be proactive and work on what is vital and less reactive, or in other words, not to be distracted by what is trivial.

Shift 7, Stop chasing: most of what we want we have. Once we wake up

We've discussed a couple of times how money is not a motivator. It's a de-motivator if we don't have enough. We've re-learnt that sometimes enough is enough. There are only so many pasta-making, bread-making and such machines that we can fit in our kitchen. This is the idea of thresholds. We need a little, but no more. So it is in nature: some salt, but no more. Some sun, but no more. So it is in our life. And once we have reached those thresholds we can turn our energy from the hunting, to the farming, to trying to get time, to enjoying them. All we need to do is wake up: so much of what we want, we desire, we seek is already available to us; just wake up and notice it.

Shift 8, the 20% we will use: Pareto in action

You may have come across the Pareto Principle at work: the 20/80 or 80/20 guide. Thus 80% of our business comes from 20% of our clients. Or 80% of our exercise benefits comes from 20% of our exercise. Ultimately Pareto reminds us that of anything we do, 20% is the key. Only 20% of our kitchen equipment do we really need, only 20% of our clothes do we wear on a day-to-day basis. Of course a worry anybody has is, *'I agree I only use 20% of the tools I have in my workshop, but very, very occasionally I do use one of the specialist tools'.* It's perhaps true, but why not hire that one when you need it? Apply this thinking to

- children's toys
- food in the cupboards
- personal clothes
- books you actually want to keep ...

and you'll find there is a huge potential for simplifying, de-cluttering and unplugging more.

And in the future: anticipate. Is this something we really want? Do we need to buy it?

THE PERFECT MURDER

HE WAS ACTUALLY PRETTY SHOCKED AT HOW MANY PEOPLE GOOGLED 'THE PERFECT MURDER'. AND THEN HE THOUGHT OF HIS BOSS.

Shift 9, Audit: what is stopping us enjoying what we have/ what are our blockers to a perfect life?

When a frustration appears, take a look at it from an unplugged point of view:

> Running around too much ... do an audit of all you do ...
>
> Spending too much ... do an audit of where the money goes ...
>
> Never in the garden ... do an audit of where you do spend your time at the weekend.

The audit is a straightforward process to return to simplicity. Kitchens get messy, bedrooms become storerooms and lives get complicated. It needn't take us long to sort that out, though.

Shift 10, Talk unplugged and introduce it to your way of being

Don't let 'unplugged' be something you try for a month. Make it a part of your routine and ritual. Make it part of your language. A term for simplification, returning to the essence. As in how could we 'unplug' our family holidays if you are feeling they have become far too expensive and starting to miss the point of what they were meant for? How could you 'unplug' your finances if you seem to have endless accounts all with passwords, pins and different T&C?

Unplugged at Home Might Mean

- The annual spring clean. Walk and work from room to room: chuck it out, recycle it, reuse it. The questions to ask: what can we recycle, reuse or chuck?

- Simplify. Why all those bank accounts? Question: what can we make even simpler?

- The family meeting to ensure maximum cooperation in the family.

- Check lists and capture lists. To ensure the next camping trip or the annual expedition to Spain is easy and trouble free.

- Having digital free places and digital free times.

- Respecting family meals
- Remembering quality of life vs. standard of living.

Unplugged at Work Might Mean

- Realising less is more: fewer meetings, fewer people in meetings, fewer slide-decks and fewer slides in those slide-decks.

- Finding the system behind the problem. There is a problem, a complaint. But what is the cause of that? You can keep focusing on individual client problems or you can get to the heart of the issue. You can keep shouting at your child for forgetting things for school or you can find some kind of system which helps them remember.

Unplugged For the Kids Might Mean

- No more 'micro scheduling' of their days
- Respecting their free time
- Allowing boredom
- Encouraging hands and heart as well as head and iPhone.

Maria

The irony of Maria's lifestyle did not amuse her one bit. Having made her money in the financial bastions of the City of London, and bailed out just before the 2008 crisis, she had initially been living the dream. The Spanish farmhouse was gorgeous. The buildings were gently restored, the land securely fenced and her vision created: a retreat for 'super stressed' business people. Hers was a premium product. To stay was expensive, her coaching and workshops priced at the top end of the market. But she had no problems filling her spaces and she knew she was very good at what she did. But her great work drew great references and great references created more business for her. And more business required extra building work and project management and a separate site and staff who unfortunately didn't have some of her perspective on what she was trying to do ...

Eighteen months on and she was more stressed than she had ever been in her City days. She wasn't sleeping well. Her personal meditations were full of turbulence. Her teaching lost its flow. Reviews became less excellent and more OK. Business dropped but there were still loans to be serviced ...

She closed for two months. Accepted no more bookings. After the last class she decided to unplug and re-boot herself. She walked the grounds, watched the sunrise and sunset, slept and meditated. She cooked good food slowly. She ate slowly. She walked slowly. Slowly but surely her body returned to balance. She sold all additional properties, one at a slight loss: but so be it. It was, after all, only money. She returned to the core farm, a small number of rooms, the occasional workshop and coaching individuals who respected her work. She managed by herself. Personal contact was restored and she put up her prices a little.

Her flow and passion returned to her teaching. She loved it. She had needed to unplug again.

A Few Questions If I May?

1. *Mmmm. I sort of like it. But shades of new age? Zen style thinking?*

And your question is? Part of unplugged thinking is to drop the label. So long as we are respecting friends, family and of course being a good citizen what matters here is what helps you live a full and happy life. It may well be different from what the crowd are doing. That's the point. It may well cause others surprise at your behaviour. They may think we are eccentric, or even downright weird. It doesn't matter. Give it a try. Forget the labels: look for the results.

2. *The unplugged approach does require the support of many others, surely? Teenagers are not always so happy with a 'stripped down' lifestyle when they compare it with what others are doing and getting. And in the commercial world everyone wants to own a bit of the plan, which can create incredible complexity. What's the best way to win someone over to this (it certainly may seem) much more radical approach?*

Most people are increasingly expressing frustration with business overload and simply have too much to do to do and too much to think about. Capture one of these moments of frustration and suggest that you would like to talk to them more about that. About how, at home, to have more time in the evening. At work, how to have more time to do a quality job on fewer projects. And then introduce a few of these ideas. You'll find people get it and people love it.

3. *With an unplugged approach am I going to miss out? What about just splashing out on the holiday of a lifetime? Or a bit of retail therapy? Or a real house just full of wonderful things collected over a lifetime?*

All fine, of course. If you are conscious of what you are doing you can still maintain the unplugged lifestyle. The unplugged approach is not austere, sterile or wary of fun or letting go. The unplugged lifestyle is so straightforward that spontaneity, the ridiculous and the odd crazy purchase are much easier to accommodate.

And Now Back To You

Unplugged is not just a set of snappy techniques: it's a whole approach and philosophy. The value and benefits of such a way of thinking are remarkable.

Unplugged starts with a balanced Personal Compass. It is supported by working on your wellness. It is completed by managing the way we think.

There are ten shifts which specifically support the unplugged methodology

1. **Compass: check, balance and lighten.** Check the six points are heading in the direction you seek. Balance each compass point against the other five to check they are aligned and mutually supporting and finally keep lightening them to avoid overload.

2. **Be here now.** Do not defer your life. Be here now. Enjoy the weather, the conversation, even the workout at the gym. Now.

3. **Less is more.** When you add something, drop something. You have finite time, accept that and realise that more enjoyment comes from doing a few things well than a roller-coaster of attempted peak experiences.

4. **Get good.** Seek understanding and expertise which gives you mastery and wisdom.

5. **Just say no.** No to too much stuff, no to too many demands, no to calls from different time zones into your evenings.

6. **Be proactive rather than reactive.** Anticipate. Pick up a couple of the time management practices. At the time period change what do I indeed to anticipate?

7. **Chase less, appreciate more.** Enjoy the journey. It is a long way to Scotland. But the road takes you through staggeringly beautiful countryside.

8. **Think Pareto.** 20% achieves a staggering amount. The dinner party does not need to be perfect. Care and attention with the food, some candles, perhaps even a bit of Sinatra. Go on: cheat on the dessert. It'll be wonderful.

9. **Audit.** Do a check list. Capture all your frustrations, such as not being able to get all the washing done. Too many books around the place. Hellish weekends. And then work on it.

10. **Live and breathe unplugged.** The more you act it, the more you will think it, the more you will live it.

YOU, ONLY BETTER • **SECTION 8** ⟶

HOW TO CREATE MASSIVE MOMENTUM BEHIND THE CHANGES YOU SEEK

You don't need to read, study or reflect any more: you have all the knowledge, ideas, techniques and shifts you need. You do need to make it all happen though. Have you ever had a New Year's resolution NOT happen? Of course: everyone has. Have you ever had a great behaviour change, such as going swimming three times a week, just somehow stop happening? Indeed. Have you ever begun to believe you can't get change to happen for you? That would be a huge shame of course.

It is possible to get the changes you seek. It is possible to get them to stick. It is possible to overcome any blocker you might meet. Here's how:

YOU
DO
NOT
NEED
APPROVAL

YOU
NEED
A
PLAN

Have a Plan

Know what you want to do and make it a clear and visible part of your daily life. A simple suggestion is to create a giant wall plan: get a piece of paper about flip-chart pad size (tape some A4 sheets together if necessary) and create a simple matrix: along the top put the topics you wish to address, e.g. career, energy, relationships, money. A good default approach is to simply put down the six compass points: career, wellness, money, relationships, fun and contribution. Then down the side, put the next 12 months. You then end up with a matrix with a box or cell for each behaviour change for each month. Now review your notes and list the key changes that you are looking for each month and write them large and bold in the box, in the cell. This plan, this matrix, should now go somewhere where you will see it every day.

Your Mission Area

A good place for it to go would be in your own working area. If you are lucky enough to have your own study or working area, place it above your desk. If not place it on the back of your bedroom door. In general only make it visible to those who will support you, but ensure it is seen by you on a regular basis. If you do have your own table and working area make it a real mission area: clear plans plus all the tools such as laptop, pens and notebook that you need. If you don't have that, then clear a drawer which is dedicated to your notebooks and current reading: get used to clearing a space at the kitchen table and quickly laying out all the equipment that you need.

Make It Easy

As each month approaches, transfer the list from the box/cell which is at the intersection of the month and the topic you are working on e.g. *November/career: discuss promotion; pay to go on course myself; consider on-line MBA* to your Master List. As you will remember, part of the Master List review is to break, break and date in order that all tasks are both time (c 45 minutes) and brain (yep, I could do that) friendly. As the month progresses the tasks can move from your open (a possibility) Master List to your daily closed (an actuality) list. You will see progress.

THERE WERE MANY WALLS IN LIFE

 SUPPORTING

 POTENTIAL

 BLOCKING

CRUMBLING

GARDEN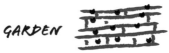

 PINK FLOYD

LEGO

HER STAGE 1 WAS TO CONCENTRATE ON THOSE THAT BLOCKED HER PROGRESS

Build Rituals

A ritual? Sure: nothing to do with reading the chicken entrails! A ritual is something which becomes automatic. We hardly need to 'think' about it, it just happens. And that's what we want for our personal change programme, our quest for the best version of ourselves. Sounds good? Absolutely. Brushing our teeth is a ritual for most of us. We don't plan it, we don't think about it, we don't worry about it, we just do it. If you are a driver, there are many rituals which were drummed into you during your training: indicate before your turn, glance over your shoulder before pulling out, check for bicycles before opening the car door on busy streets etc. Our goal is to get the change we want to become that easy, that wired in. Regular following of the same mechanics will enable that to happen, so do not be concerned that at the moment you have to think about the changes to make them happen. You once had to do that with teeth brushing, car driving: it was conscious competence. Stick at it and it will become unconscious competence: a ritual.

Bash the Blockers

Of course sorting the mechanics, i.e. the wall planner, the Master List, and making them all a routine, even better a ritual is brilliant. There is still mindset to contend with: the fact that what is logical is not always enough to encourage the shift. What is common sense is not always common practice. We need to contend with the blockers that can occur. Now some of these we have touched on before, but in this session we will discuss them more thoroughly and conveniently capture them in one place:

No time

'I don't have enough time, you say.'

There never will be enough time: accept that. It's about choices. Don't wait for time: there won't be a space. You have to create time. Take your diary and schedule it in. No time next week you say? Nor the week after? OK: so schedule it in for the week after that ... Remember the big rocks in the jar story?

NEWTON STARTED HERE

MICHELANGELO STARTED HERE

EINSTEIN STARTED HERE

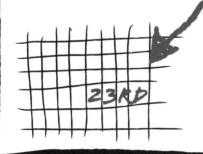

23RD

YOU STARTED HERE

No support

'The trouble is, this is just seen as my thing. Not exactly selfish but a bit, considering all the other things we have to do.'

But, you say, I would love to do that. I'd love to get on my bicycle every Saturday but I have got family commitments and those all come first. Mmmm, but they don't have to come first always. Of course. But remember if you do not do a bit of work on yourself you will stop growing and if you are not growing you will not be the effective parent, partner, leader, employee that you so wish to be. This is not selfish, it's eminently sensible but it will require some conversation, some working on the 5As. Thus, you could agree with your partner, your kids, that certain Saturdays or certain parts of Saturdays will be yours.

No money

'Look there is simply no spare cash at the moment.'

You'd love to de-clutter, but you need storage and have no money. You'd love to start your own business but you have no money for the initial stock. You'd love to do more with the kids at the weekend but you have no money for museums and movies. There are a couple of options. One of course is to get on top of that part of your compass: get your finances sorted and then maybe there will be some money available. But perhaps a more creative point of view is to ask:

- Where can we find some very cheap even free storage? Thus charity shops and re-cycling schemes.

- Or to ask, how can I start up my business with just the (very little) money that I do have?

No energy

This is crucial. So go right back to the wellness compass point and work on that. Once you are looking after yourself and addressing the key areas your energy will return. Once you start having success you will find that you feel you have more energy anyway.

Not motivated

Don't wait until you are motivated: start and then you will be motivated.

Not now

It won't get any easier. The children will always have their challenges; there will always be demands on your money. Start getting in control now. Start sorting things out now.

What will people think?

Don't worry. Few will support you, sadly. But that doesn't stop you getting on with things: you do not need their approval.

I need (an iPad/my own area/less of a commute/...)

No you don't. You are procrastinating.

Watch Your Language

Don't label yourself: *'I'll never be good enough for promotion'.* It's simply not true. But if you say it to yourself enough it can become reality.

Keep Your Energy High

Energy and enthusiasm are contagious: they will win supporters. Energy can push through the barriers of negativity, get you out of bed in the morning and cause you to make 20 more phone calls and win the business. Look after yourself.

Only Share with Supporters

Share your goals with those who will support you. They may still have concerns or feedback for you. But they do fundamentally believe in you.

Find a Buddy

And take the above idea even further: agree to meet perhaps once a week for 60 minutes with someone else who is working on their career or health or writing or ... And support each other, cajole each other and be inspired by each other's progress.

Create a Learning Team

And take the above idea even further and find two other people and set up a learning team which meets once a month. Each person contributes some ideas and in consequence receives some ideas.

Read for Inspiration

Start with my blog (http://blog.strategicedge.co.uk/). Find other blogs. Start a reading list. Always have some source of daily inspiration to feed the mind and thus the body. In particular, study the A to Z of *You, Only Better* every day (see next chapter).

Focus On What Is Working

At the end of each month, do a bit of a review: what worked? What worked less well? Anything a bit of a disaster? Focus first on what's working and build upon that. Perhaps if you work on things at different times of the day you get more done. Perhaps now that your energy is building you find you can do anything. Build on what's working. Now look at what's not gone to plan and how you could do that differently next month.

Make Change the Norm

Start to see this change programme as something which is going to be the norm for you, i.e. there will always be a wall planner, you will always be working on something.

Ben

Ben was a cynic. A cynic who lived in Quebec City. He had escaped his native New York five years earlier and loved being closer to nature, spending the weekend in the wilds and being in a place he felt was a lot more 'real'. The 'can do' nature of New Yorkers sometimes got him down. Of course Canadians were very practical and self-sufficient too, but ... well it was different.

He was a cynic about change and goals and all that stuff. He'd set enough of them over the years: they never worked. He'd tried various methodologies, even affirmations: what a joke they were. He'd even had a personal coach for about three months. But nothing, nothing had ever got him the change he really wanted.

But deep down he wasn't that comfortable. The cynicism he recognised in himself caused him to not enjoy much of life which, with a simple shift in view point, he might change very easily. Cynicism was really damaging his current relationship with a very loving girl from Montreal. Cynicism was holding him back at work. And deep down what he was wrestling with he knew – it had been a big epiphany on one of those big US 'ra ra' personal development, fire-walking seminars – he knew his cynicism was fear. Fear of realising who he was and what he might accomplish.

After one fabulous weekend of canoeing, on the two-hour drive back to Quebec City he considered why goals didn't work for him: career, making money etc. And yet he had actually achieved a lot: the move to Canada had been major change. Becoming a canoeing coach was hard work.

He got it: with the former he had simply not allowed a blocker. With the latter he had just accepted the blockers too quickly. And what caused his blockers? His cynicism.

He agreed with himself to see what dropping cynicism might do on his other goals.

Three months later, Ben had promotion, was earning 12% more money and his relationship with girlfriend Ava was better than ever.

A Few Questions If I May?

1. How do you get those who are close to you to be supporter of the changes you are making? My girlfriend just worries that my new career plans are a big mistake.

By talking to them. By thanking them for their concerns. By responding to some of their concerns. And by reminding them there are some things you just have to do. If you talk enough nothing need be a compromise but something which is good for both of you.

2. Three children and a job with international travel. Where will I find the time for changes?

By making the changes small and easy. And any large and tough change can be broken down into something which is small and easy.

3. Can You, Only Better become a selfish quest?

Oh, you're in a philosophical mood! Of course it can. We are destined to grow, find out who we are and make the most of our time on the planet. But it's important that we respect those who are on that path with us: friends and family. Employers and colleagues. But respecting such thoughts and demands need not limit us: it simply cautions us and that is no bad thing.

And Now Back To You

1. **Have a plan and work that plan:** make the plan big, bold visible and manageable.

2. **Create your own personal 'mission' area,** even if you are working from a plastic box.

3. **Make it easy.** Transfer those big rocks to your Master List. Review the Master List and break big tasks down so that they are brain and time friendly.

4. **Build rituals** so that the change enhancing processes become the norm.

5. **Bash the blockers** from 'no time' to 'I need ...'.

6. **Focus on what is working.**

7. **Make change the norm.**

ONE
OF
THE
FEW
WATER
MOLECULES
WHO
WONDERED
WHAT
LIFE
AT
THE
EDGE
WAS
REALLY
LIKE

YOU, ONLY BETTER • *SECTION 9* $\longrightarrow$

THE
A TO Z
OF YOU,
ONLY
BETTER

Let's now summarise all we have learnt, but let's 'cut' it in a different way: The A to Z of *You, Only Better*. 26 bite-sized pieces of knowledge, behaviour tips and inspiration.

How To Use the A to Z

- Focus on one letter per day. You could be linear and simply work your way through the alphabet in sequence.

- Or you could just randomly choose a number 1 to 26 and then see what letter that is and work on it.

- You could photocopy these pages of the book for your personal use and create some simple A to Z flash cards to carry around and re-read at a quiet moment.

- You could introduce the ideas to a team meeting or to your family.

A Attention

In essence: **nothing happens without attention**. It's where the art of creating *You, Only Better* starts; Woody Allen famously said *'80% of success is turning up'*. Attention is like the sweeping search-light of the prison camp escape films: where the search-light lands is what we notice, all else is darkness. Turn your search-light to where you want change. And what is the search-light? Three things: dedicated time, dedicated energy and dedicated attitude. Dedicated time? We work ON ourselves. Dedicated energy: super wellness directed to what we want. Dedicated attitude? The best empowering beliefs wrapped around what we seek to happen.

'I believe attention is the most powerful tool of the human spirit. We can enhance or augment our attention with practices like meditation or exercise, diffuse it with technologies like e-mail and Blackberries, or alter it with pharmaceuticals. In the end we are fully responsible for how we choose to use this extraordinary tool.' Linda Stone

B Belief

Learn the following mantra; it may be all you need to ensure that you are consistently successful in creating a new you.

A *You, Only Better*. **Your beliefs create your behaviours which in turn create your results**. Understand, really understand, this point and you have the fast-track route to creating a new version of you.

Drop and discard the limiting beliefs, the less than helpful beliefs and focus on the empowering beliefs, the enlivening beliefs, the ones which help you grow.

Here are some useful beliefs or mindsets to adopt:

I can
No failure: only feedback
I make the real world
I choose
There's always a way.

'Running has always been more of a mental problem than a physical problem to me.' Roger Bannister.

C Compass

Compass time is time which is important and investing, e.g. strategic planning, taking a proper lunch-break or having a proper conversation with one of the children. Compass time is where you work ON your life, ON your business, ON your health. Clock time is important and urgent, e.g. responding to a crisis, paying a bill. Clock time is where you get caught up IN your business, IN your life, IN the day to day crises. Clock time is more dependent upon our reptile or survival brain. Compass time requires us to engage our human/ higher brain. We **choose** compass time; clock time drives us. Compass time is where the amazing breakthroughs are made: choose it more often.

Check your compass to invest in:
Your **career**
Your **health**
Sorting your **finances**
Improving your **relationships**

Manage your compass time on a day-to-day basis by running a **Master List**, a dedicated list of not only what you have to do but also what you want to do. Not only short-term, but long-term. Not only now and pragmatic but also 'wow' and visionary.

'You are the storyteller of your own life and you can create your own legend, or not.' Isabel Allende.

Decision

Make the best possible decisions by (1) having full awareness of all of the issues (2) making the initial decision through a variety of techniques such as reflection and incubation, or T-bar with pros and cons, or brainstorming (3) allow some reflection time (4) then make the final decision remembering that a decision is not a decision until an action has been taken.

Your path to *You, Only Better* will require decisions; ensure your decisions involve an immediate action to create momentum.

Not just 'I have given up smoking', but *current packet crushed and binned*.
Not just 'I will save more', but *standing order from direct account to savings account completed, signed and sent off*.
Not just 'I will be more assertive', but *meeting booked with manager to resolve a few issues*.

'Whatever you can do, or dream you can, begin it! Boldness has genius, magic and power in it. Begin it now.' Goethe

Emotional Intelligence

When we think about truly effective people we notice that they are able to connect with other people and they are good listeners. They have resilience and they are happy to lead. These 'soft' skills are what are known as Emotional Intelligence (EQ). Of course such soft skills are not enough: the receptionist must not only be friendly and warm but he/she must know how to produce the security badges quickly and effectively. The Project Manager must be able to produce an accurate Gannt chart as well as coach and motivate and listen to fresh suggestions. The former competencies are often known as the 'EQ' competencies. The latter, the IQ competencies. To be truly effective, to be truly successful, we need to address both IQ and EQ. But here's something we all know: in the star performers, be they receptionists or project managers, it's the EQ which makes the real difference.

'For star performance in all fields, emotional competence is twice as important as purely cognitive abilities.' Daniel Goleman

Fear

Fear is an immensely powerful state; the goal though is not to remove it, nor reduce it, but to channel it. The fear of the presentation should ensure the work is put in. The fear of the start up should ensure the right questions are asked. The fear of the marathon should ensure the training is done. Much fear is a hangover from an earlier period in our evolution. It kicks in with change or newness or a difficult conversation. Earlier in our evolution such incidents could well have been life-threatening. Now they are part of our growth and fear needs to be accepted and only acted upon in truly frightening situations.

Susan Jeffers puts it nicely: *'Feel the fear and do it anyway'.*

Goal-Seeking Formula

You know what? There is a formula for *You, Only Better*! Follow it and success will be yours:

Step 1: decide what the new version of you is EXACTLY: be precise. Not 'wealthy', but £0.5M in assets by 35th birthday. Write it down, draw a picture and make it as 'sensory rich' as possible.

Step 2: get a strategy from a practitioner: someone who has done it. Ring them up, get their book. Pay for an hour of their time, go on a course. Ask them another question, go on another course, get another hour's coaching. Follow exactly what they did to lose weight, make money, get rid of stress, get their book published ...

Step 3: use their strategy. If successful: great. If not, it's feedback and you need to try again (persevere) and/or adapt the strategy.

Step 4: success will be yours.

'Success is the maximum utilisation of the ability that you have.' **Zig Ziglar**

Hero

Heroes have the courage to do what is necessary when it is necessary. What if you were a hero? What if you were able to step above the daily excuses? What if you were that person you want to become? What if you became *You, Only Better*.

A hero gives ATTENTION to what is important.
A hero BELIEVES they can make a difference.
A hero sets his/her COMPASS.
A hero makes DECISIONS and takes ACTION.
A hero uses their EMOTIONAL INTELLIGENCE as well as just their pure 'smartness'.
A hero transforms FEAR.
A hero uses the GOAL-SEEKING FORMULA to create a new even better version of themselves.

Being a hero is not about arrogance. It is not about seeking celebrity. It is not about being 'right'. It's about releasing your true potential.

'A hero is a man who would argue with the gods.' **Norman Mailer**

Internally Referenced

When you are internally referenced, you stay true to your inner principles and what is truly important. If you want to do more studying, you'll do it, despite the cynical comments. If you want to give up smoking, you will do it, despite the fuss. Of course, don't be selfish or ignore feedback.

If you are *externally referenced*, you will be swayed by any comment. You will miss out on some of your dreams and you may never discover the true you. Staying internally referenced is tough, very tough. We all want to be liked and one of the easiest ways to do that is NOT to rock the boat;

the shame is that that approach will take us away, far away from the best version of ourselves.

'I'm just an individual who doesn't feel that I need to have somebody qualify my work in any particular way. I'm working for me.' David Bowie

Journey

Your happiness, your growth, will depend as much if not more upon the journey you make to your goal than on the destination, the goal, itself. Journey thinking: enjoy now; learn as you go; measure growth and investment; do less – achieve more; focus on your compass and less on the clock. Journey thinking: what am I learning, looking out of the window, smelling the flowers, having time for conversations, listening and learning. Journey thinking: wherever I am is the perfect place for me to be.

'Time you enjoy wasting, was not wasted.' John Lennon

'Killer App'

There is one ultimate, definitive, 'killer app'. One superb, easy, no-nonsense way of getting the success you want. And that is JFDI: Just F***ing Do It.

There comes a point when there are no more techniques to study, no more books to read, enough courses have been attended, enough planning done. It's time to get on with it, to do it.

Go on: JFDI! You have no time? Make a choice. You have no energy? Work on your wellness programme. You think not now? There may not be an opportunity tomorrow. You worry what people will think? Who cares? It may not work? But it might! You don't have the resources you need? Find them, anywhere. You're stuck. Change your state: go for a walk, talk, stretch … You'd love to but … How about you'd love to and …

JFDI! Anon

Lifelong Learning

An important aspect of 'compass' time or 'on' time is personal investment: health, relationships and of course learning.

Your future employability is a function of your current learning. Many people spend more on their car than they do on their brain. Decide now to invest at least 2% of your income in your personal development. Go on courses, read widely, learn from those with great skills, set up a learning team, carry and use a notebook. And use life as the most amazing personal development programme ever. Learning need not be expensive. Learning need not take time. But learning does need a decision to do it.

'Forget to remember the stuff you don't need any more.' Richard Bandler

Motivation

Don't wait until you are motivated: you might wait a long time. Start: and then you get motivated. Look for the intrinsic worth in any task, ensure that you are in great state, seek clarity of what it is you want. De-clutter and get organised. Walk tall and be grateful. Look for the motivation which is deep within you. Attempt to become less and less dependent upon external carrots, be they money, a holiday, a trip to the movies. Become fired up by you: your plans, your achievements, by *You, Only Better*.

'The greatest danger for most of us is not that our aim is too high and we miss it, but too low and we reach it.' Michelangelo

Niche

Identify your niche, your own bit of the Universe. Your niche is your specialist area, your area of expertise, your passion. Because it is your passion, you tend to enjoy working in that area. Because you enjoy working in that area you tend to be good at it. Because you are good at it, you tend to be well paid for it. Hey presto! Success.

But do remember, most of us are born generalists. There are prodigies of course: those are the bell-curve extremities. In any field they exist: tax management, rock 'n roll or being a cool town guide: those whose gene combinations create something pretty rare.

For the majority of us though, we need to regularly remind ourselves that it's not nature or nurture. It's **nurture your nature**. Work at stuff. Work at everything until passions, loves and talents are revealed. They won't be easy to decipher and despite exhortations to 'follow your passion' they won't be easy to identify amongst the smoke and mirrors of what you are paid to do, have to do, fancy doing and what is currently cool to do. So work and work hard at everything you do because **you are one of the few in your field who are astoundingly good at what you do**: *you simply have to find that field*. And when you do, you receive the highest and most just reward for the hard work and accomplishment of mastery. **Freedom.**

'Follow your bliss.' Joseph Campbell

Organisation

Being organised enables you to be the best version of you. Being organised requires three things: firstly the mental approach to work 'on' yourself, i.e. to be an investor; secondly a simple practical management approach, i.e. to use the Master List and thirdly a working environment which is conducive to the best kind of thinking.

Plan your day and week to include both in and on time. Create a Master List and review it on a daily basis. Create your own 'mission control' area. Put the three together and you'll be organised.

'Have nothing in your house that you do not know to be useful, or believe to be beautiful.' William Morris

Passion

Passion comes easily when you are the best version of you. Passion is created by working on you, so that you are at your best. Passion comes from working on what you are best at. Passion comes from continuing to grow. Passion comes from inside you. Passion is elusive yet wonderful when you have it. Passion is a quest not an expectation. Passion is a reward not a right. Passion will appear as the A to Z falls in to place.

'Whatever you do, do it with passion.' Carlos Castaneda

Quantum Thinking

Journalists describe a big change as a 'quantum change', e.g. *'there has been a quantum breakthrough in medical research'*. Physicists remind us that 'quantum' is a small and discrete change.

So, what is quantum *thinking*? It's a small, discrete change which yields powerful results, for example from the usual strategy of *spend, then save* to the more powerful one of **save, then spend.** Small change, but very powerful results. Or from *I can be a coder earning a lot of money* to an artist who is poor but happy **to I can be a coder working a few days week and an artist producing great work as I am relaxed about whether I sell anything or not ...**

'You can analyse the past, but you have to design the future.' Edward De Bono

Rainmaker

A rainmaker is someone who can make it happen. Despite all the challenges, he/she makes it rain. A rainmaker is resourceful, a rainmaker is 'can do', a rainmaker sees possibilities, a rainmaker has a plan. Everybody appreciates the rainmaker. Every town, every village and every firm needs a rainmaker. The good news is no dances nor chicken entrails are needed to be a good rainmaker: just a decision to be *You, Only Better*. Be a rainmaker.

'You are only as good as your last gig.' Tom Peters

Success

Complete this sentence:

Success for me is ...

Now put that somewhere where it is visible to you every day. Success is what you want: *You, Only Better*. It is not what your mum says. It is not what the conference dictates. It is not defined in this book. Success must be defined by you.

But along the way there will be plateaus or points where nothing seems to be improving. And there will also be dips or points where things seem to be getting worse. A plateau is merely consolidation. A dip is merely re-wiring.

'Love the dip and love the plateau.' George Leonard

Today

Today is a really good time to take an action, to start working on some changes you desire, to create your definitive personal development plan, to ... Yesterday is learning and reflection. Tomorrow is planning. Today is action: today is where *You, Only Better* is created.

'Learn from yesterday, live for today, hope for tomorrow. The important thing is not to stop questioning.' Albert Einstein

Uncertainty

Will our new business be successful? Nobody knows. Will she accept the request to go to the cinema? Who knows? Will regular exercise help my knee? Not even the doctor absolutely definitely knows! Things are uncertain. We plan to reduce uncertainty, but we must accept that looking for 100% assurance could be a blocker to what we are really after.

On our path to a new version of you, i.e. *You, Only Better*, we must be able to accept uncertainty. Certainty is only one path. Uncertainty gives access to other potential options. Uncertainty keeps us grounded.

'Uncertainty is a sign of humility, and humility is just the ability or the willingness to learn.' Charlie Sheen

Vision

Take an A4 piece of paper. Turn it landscape. In the top right-hand corner write today's date + 3 years. Now DRAW your vision: how do you **want** things to be? Just DRAW.

When you have finished, put it somewhere where you will see it every day. And act upon it.

'Dream as if you will live forever. Live as if you will die today.' James Dean

Who?

Who can help you? Who can help you on your path? Do not be afraid to ask: that's all it takes for many people. And those who say no often simply mean not now; ask them when is a good time? And what are you asking for? Their wisdom, their tips, their nuggets, their top tips. Stuff which will help you fast-track your own plans.

Go on, who can help? And in return of course, help others.

'And in the end. The love you take is equal to the love you make.'
Lennon and McCartney

Multiply

Multiply the impact of several aspects. How about giving your health *attention*, making a clear decision and using the *goal-seeking* formula, i.e. A x D x G? Or F x L x P?

'Talent is in the choices.' Robert De Niro

Yin and Yang

Success is so often the power of complementary forces. Without failure, how can you be successful? Without the journey, how can we get to the destination?

Not just masculine, but *feminine*, too.
Not just certainty, but *uncertainty*, too.

'I'm very happy your work is going so well for you. I'd just like you to know that you are the most boring man that I know.' Elizabeth, wife of Charles Handy

Zen and the Art of *You, Only Better*

It's surprisingly easy to be the best version of you: *You, Only Better*. A little focus, a few shifts and everything you seek is yours.

'There is no way to happiness. Happiness is the way.' Dalai Lama

Jane

Jane was stuck, absolutely stuck. Her days were exhausting as she travelled between the stores for which she was responsible across her part of the country. If she wasn't in the car she was in a meeting and if she wasn't in a meeting, she was part of a conference call. And if she wasn't doing something work related she was managing a crisis with her children. Jane felt stuck, absolutely stuck. She needed to kick-start some changes and so on a whim she took five random cards from her A to Z pack which she had made and lined them up on the kitchen table in alphabetical order; she had once read a book on synchronicity and thought maybe a bit of 'nature support' could help her.

She opened her eyes to discover the letters D, E, G, L and P.

Mmm...

Decision. Sadly this was a very good prompt for her. She was trying hard. She was listening to audio business books in the car. She was writing things down in her notebook. But she was not making decisions. She was absorbing material but not making decisions. Why not? Simply because they were not real enough for her to act upon. 'Get fit.' 'Save more money.' Too abstract and too general.

She got it: more detailed, specific actions. OK: here was her first. To take a real action every day that helped improve either her life or that of her children or that of anyone she knew.

Emotional Intelligence. She loved this idea. Always had from when she had first been introduced to it. She now needed to use it. Push back on some of the bullies she reported in to. Get some of her clients to listen a bit better. Yes: emotional intelligence was her power weapon, her power tool. She was going to multiply D by E. Clear decisions and engaging her EQ.

Goal-Seeking Formula. This was critical. She did set goals, but didn't make decisions, and the Goal-Seeking Formula was brilliant and showed exactly how to do it. She currently had about 5 or 6 critical goals; she now needed to find and identify the relevant strategies. And if she multiplied D by E by G or great decisions taken with emotional intelligence to execute the essential goals then she would be able to get exactly what she sought.

Life-long Learning. Initially she was a little disappointed by this card. She felt this was the one thing she was already doing very well: learning. After all none of the rest of her colleagues did any learning apart from the mandatory three days per year. But as she reflected she realised that maybe this card, this letter, was reminding her that she did need to do some learning but a different kind of learning. And she went right back to a skill which she had never really been accomplished at school: knitting. And that got her into a knitting circle which was fun, relaxing and she was also producing a wonderful hand-made knit for her daughter. Multiplying D by E by G by L was creating some astonishing results.

Passion. How she had hated that term the first time through the A to Z. Because she simply didn't have it. She knew people who did but she didn't. And she wanted it. But those five cards had helped her regain it. It had been sparked by the knitting and after such sessions she had felt energised enough to NOT sit up all night doing work e-mail but sit and read or talk with the family. As a consequence she slept better and was far more effective the next day and slowly but surely she found her passion for the job was coming back which meant – not surprisingly – she was getting the results she needed. And she wanted. She won Regional Director of the Year. D by E by G by L by P!

Your Very Own Set of A to Z Cards

By the way, if you want your very own set of the A to Z cards they are available on amazon.co.uk.

And Now Back To You

It's time now to get the A to Z of *You, Only Better* to become something which is not just sitting in a book, but something you live and breathe. It's now all down to you!

About the Author

There is no more book, but of course your journey continues. Here is the simplest of ways to get a little daily inspiration to help you with the execution of your plans: check in to my blog as I post most days. It is found at:

http://blog.strategicedge.co.uk/

Nicholas Bate

Nicholas Bate is passionate about supporting people to ensure they realise and *release* their true and full potential. It is the simple purpose of his organisation, Strategic Edge and his teaching, consulting and writing.

After a career in sales and marketing in the IT industry, culminating in leading sector marketing for Research Machines, Oxford, UK, Nicholas launched Strategic Edge. A small, premium consultancy, Strategic Edge specialises in creating long-term competitive advantage for its clients including Microsoft, Starbucks, Marks and Spencer, The BBC, Royal Sun Alliance and Oxfam amongst others.

A pioneering 'thought leader', Nicholas has introduced and worked with his clients on a range of simple yet powerful concepts which help with challenges such as ever-demanding productivity, work/life balance and new routes to innovation.

He has designed, written and teaches six highly innovative courses: Personal Excellence; Brilliant at the Basics of Selling; Personal Presence; Instant MBA; How To Boost Your Creativity; and The Five Choices of Outstanding Customer Service.

Consistently rated as an inspirational yet highly pragmatic key-note speaker, Nicholas teaches around the world (UK and continental Europe; USA and Canada; Asia) and is particularly skilled at working in an experiential and engaging manner. He works as a coach to many senior people in the industry in areas such as presentation skills, work/life balance and creativity.

He is the author of 15 acclaimed books, all available on Amazon:

Being The Best: how to realise and release your true potential

Do What You Want: the book that shows you how to create a career you will love

How To Be Brilliant: characteristics of excellence

Brilliant at The Basics of Business 100: brilliant business in 100 short, sharp tips

Love Presenting; Hate (badly used) PowerPoint: enough said

Be Bold 101

Professionalism 101

Get A Life: how to achieve the work–life balance you are seeking

JfDI: Just Do It: the definitive guide to enabling your vision

Unplugged: the time for personal re-invention is now

Beat the Recession: a blueprint for success in tough times

Have it Your Way: how to influence

Instant MBA: MBA thinking, quickly

BlackBerry Fool: how to use the clever device with intelligence

How to Sell and Market your Way out of this Recession

Plus a range of 'mini-books' available directly from Nicholas: Morph, Revolution 101, Celeb Productivity, Boost Your Productivity, Priceless 101, A–Z of Excellence cards, A–Z of Sales cards, Moleskin Meditations, Why We Love The Beatles, Appunti, The Breakthrough 53, Outrageous 101, Vroom cards.

He has an active and inspirational yet highly practical blog with a worldwide following: http://blog.strategicedge.co.uk/

To contact Nicholas, ring the Strategic Edge office at: +44 1865 764953 or mail him directly via Nicholas.bate@strategicedge.co.uk.

Picture credits

P3 Autumn sunrise – © Mordolff/istockphoto.com
P39 Kneading and making yeast dough – © Melhi/istockphoto.com
P57 Coins of the world II – © Dizzy/istockphoto.com
P89 Sky – © Neomistyle/istockphoto.com
P106 Phrenology head – © Themoog/istockphoto.com
P144 Rural Spain – © Filo/istockphoto.com
P159 Kayaking on Emerald Lake – © Antb/istockphoto.com

All original illustrations by Nicholas Bate

LIFE IS GOOD

Life is good. Rarely easy. Often funny, outrageous, wonderful, thought-provoking. At times exasperating, doubt-inducing, desperately worrying and frightening. But deep down: life is good. Life lacks enough clear maps, timetables and simple instruction guides; it appears at times to deliberately mislead you and steer you down a few side paths until you hit the clear empty highway and can begin to motor. It introduces you to plenty of case studies, odd-ball characters and crazy schemes but it does provide books, rock 'n roll and one or two awesome HBO series. Oh and decent coffee if you choose carefully and allow the water to cool a little. *Life is surely worth one or two hiccups in order to be exposed to the entire collection of Beatles masterpieces.* Life is rarely explicit: where, after all is the fun in that? Life will introduce love and your head and heart will seek to explode. Life will take it away; yes, just like that. Life will create mind-boggling amounts of energy, focus and sheer joy and then bring you down to earth in stale sheets and aching limbs with the flu. Life will rain on your parade. The bowl of cherries will be 'temporarily unavailable'. The central line will be down, again. Life will cause tears. Of joy and of heart-breaking worry. Life never promised to be easy but tearing open the packet, getting stuck in and working hard allows overall, on balance, considering all the various parameters and listening to all the subject matter experts and taking appropriate due diligence ... **life is good.** *Man, damn good.*